It's Great to Be a Girl!

A Guide to Your Changing Body

Dannah Gresh
& Suzy Weibel

HARVEST HOUSE PUBLISHERS
EUGENE, OREGON

Cover and interior design by www.DesignByJulia, Woodland Park, Colorado
Cover illustration by Julia Ryan / DesignByJulia.com
Interior spot illustrations and doodles: Julia Ryan and Shutterstock.com
Illustrations by Andy Mylin: 10–11, 55
Charts: © Shutterstock: 81: Basheera Designs; 100: BlueRingMedia
Interior photos (numbers indicate page location):
    © Shutterstock, photographers as follows: 8: Rob Marmion; 18: DnDavis;
    31, 59, 109: Blend Images; 33: Gina Santa Maria; 45, 87: Michelle D. Milliman;
    48: Creatista; 57, 74, 83: glenda; 66: Raisa Kanarev; 72: jackhollingsworth.com;
    91: @erics; 99: Horst Petzold; 115: Ken Hurst
    © Dan Seifert, Stone House Photography: 58, 107
    © Steve Tressler, Mountainview Studios: 27, 61, 77, 112
    © Getty Images: 94

IT'S GREAT TO BE A GIRL!
Copyright © 2015 Dannah Gresh and Suzy Weibel
Published by Harvest House Publishers
Eugene, Oregon 97408
www.harvesthousepublishers.com

    Library of Congress Cataloging-in-Publication Data
    Gresh, Dannah, author.
    It's great to be a girl! / Dannah Gresh.
        pages cm.—(Secret keeper girl series)
    ISBN 978-0-7369-6007-6 (pbk.)
    ISBN 978-0-7369-6008-3 (eBook)
    1. Teenage girls—Religious life—Juvenile literature. 2. Teenage girls—Conduct of life—Juvenile literature. 3. Beauty, Personal—Biblical teaching—Juvenile literature. 4. Puberty—Biblical teaching—Juvenile literature. I. Title.
    BV4551.3G73 2015
    248.8'33—dc23

                                                    2014032372

Printed in the United States of America
19 20 21 22 23 / VP-DBJ/ 12 11 10 9

To our moms, Kay Barker and Sharon Dunton

Thank you for showing us what it means to be a girl, for teaching us to do so with dignity, and for never getting lost in the process. You continue to be such great leaders for us to follow!

Love, your girls, Dannah and Suzy

It's great to be a girl!

Oh, really? There are some days we might argue that with you. Girls have to carry things in their purses that boys will just never have to carry. For that matter, what's so great about having to carry a purse? (We take that back. Purses are fun fashion items!)

But it *is* great to be a girl, and we want to say thank you to some of our favorite girls, including Julia Ryan, our awesome Secret Keeper Girl designer. Julia loves art and has made a career of designing books like the one you have in your hands right now. She also loves her home high in the Colorado mountains—and she thinks it's great to be a girl!

We really appreciate our great team of girls at Harvest House—LaRae Weikert and Barb Sherrill—as well as the guys—Terry Glaspey, Paul Gossard, and Gene Skinner. You'd be reading this on a computer screen (not nearly as fun) if it weren't for them!

We also want to thank some girls who pal around with us all the time—Eileen and Aleigha hold down the office in Pennsylvania all year round. Eileen is always ready for visitors with a jar of chocolate on her desk, and guess what Aleigha is up to? She's about to become the new Gresh girl! That's right, she's marrying Dannah's son Robby this summer! Aleigha and Eileen make sure everything Secret Keeper Girl does runs smoothly, and boy are they good at it!

And we are super grateful for our girls on the road—Charmaine, Ashley, Colleen, and Kristyna. These are the girls you meet when you come to our shows. Day after day they set up that show, hop on stage, make you laugh, and lead you in worship. Then they get to do their favorite thing of all—they get to meet you.

And you are our favorite girls of all. Thank *you* for coming to see us, loving to learn, and proclaiming with us that it's *great* to be a girl!

CONTENTS

A Note from Dannah and Suzy

Cue the dramatic, tension-building music. A mysterious adventure is about to begin, and the star is you. But then again…you might begin to wonder if that's actually you when you look in the mirror.

- ♥ Your body may be thickening.

- ♥ You're growing taller by the second. (Or are the boys shrinking?)

- ♥ The hair on your head may be getting thicker or more oily.

- ♥ Hair is appearing in the most surprising places.

- ♥ You're growing breasts.

- ♥ You're starting to sweat more and even smell a little different (and it's not always that pleasant).

[Welcome to puberty!]

We promise—that really is you in the mirror. Becoming a woman requires you to go through this thing called puberty, and we're here as your tour guides. (Your tour will be even better if you ask your mom to be a tour guide too, using the book *Raising Body-Confident Daughters*. Adding one of those eight great dates after each of the eight meditations in this book will bring extra power and wisdom to your experience.) We will teach you how to know and love your body. God says your body is super important and meaningful.

The Bible has *a lot* to say about your body and its purpose. We'll get a grasp on that, and we'll learn some really cool stuff about practical issues—hair care, food, exercise, and more. Of course, the Bible doesn't specifically address those everyday issues very much, but we've dug deep, and we'll share with you God's instructions for taking care of this amazing vessel he has created—your body!

[You've got this, Secret Keeper Girl!]

How to Use the Bible Study

You can do this Secret Keeper Girl Bible study all alone if you want to. But we have some other ideas for you in case you'd like to be creative:

Mother-Daughter Bible Study

Your mom will learn as much as you will. You see, we aren't the teachers—God is. His Spirit is fully capable of helping your mom to meditate in a way that teaches her as she leads you. To do this with your mom, just get two copies and dig in. You can do it once a week, or you can do it every day for a week.

Small Group or Sunday School

How fun would it be to discuss all the great things you learn each week? You can do that by grabbing a group of friends to do this with. Do it after school once a week or in Sunday school every Sunday. We like to keep things simple with Secret Keeper Girl Bible studies, so you really don't need any extra books. If you're the leader, just select one appropriate question from each of the three sections:

Look Inside Yourself

Reach Up to Talk to GOD

DIG IN to Study

Be sure to enjoy some fun snacks at the beginning and to end in prayer!

Getting Ready to DIG IN to Bible Study

This Secret Keeper Girl series uses the powerful skill of *meditation* to help you dig in to God's Word. So before you get into the great subject of your body, we'd like to take a little time to introduce you to meditation. (If you've done another book in the series, you can skip this if you want. But it will be great review—it offers new verses to help you practice meditation, and it will get you kick-started on this biblical journey through puberty.)

What Is Meditation?

You might think meditation is a crazy, weird thing you do while sitting cross-legged in a yoga position and humming. That's not true at all. That kind of meditation is just a sad fake for God's original. Let's see if we can help you get an idea of what God thinks meditation should look like.

Some Christians are so rigid about praying all the time that they never take time to study! Other Christians are so consumed with studying, studying, studying the Bible that they don't take time to pray!

Some Christians are really rigid about studying, studying, studying the Bible!

Some Christians are so consumed with praying all the time, they never study!

STUDIER

PRAY-ER

The risk for the **studier** is that her faith gets stuck in her head. She never has the heart to follow God because she is always arguing about or defending what she *thinks* about God.

The risk for the **pray-er** is that her faith is all about her heart. She makes decisions to follow God based on how she *feels* and forgets to think about what God has already told her in his written Word. (God will never ask you to do something that disagrees with the Bible.)

But then there's a third type of person. A **meditator** studies the Bible and then asks God to help her understand it while she prays. A wise pastor once told me (Dannah) that meditation is what happens when studying and praying crash into each other!

We want to teach you to meditate. You need these things:

MEDITATOR

1. Your Bible. You won't actually use it a lot because we're printing most of the verses you'll need right in this book. But we want you to get in the habit of having your very own treasured Bible on hand!

2. This copy of the Secret Keeper Girl book *It's Great to Be a Girl!*

3. Some colored markers or pencils.

These are your meditation tools. Got 'em? Okay— let's get them warmed up by practicing some meditation.

DIG IN by Studying Psalm 139:13-16

Throughout this book, you'll see this symbol inviting you to "dig in." This means you are about to *study* God's Word, kind of like an archeologist studies the ground to uncover mysteries, secrets, and stories. So, plop on your hard hat 🪖 and get ready to dig. Let's give it a try, okay?

Let's do a little digging to see if God really does want us to practice meditation. After all, you shouldn't take our word for it.

Psalm 139 talks a lot about your body. Actually, it's written by King David, and he's writing about his own body. But we know these things are also true about our bodies. Circle the word "you" or "your" with your pink marker every time it shows up.

➤ Psalm 139:13-16

For you formed my inward parts;

you knitted me together in my mother's womb.

I praise you, for I am fearfully and wonderfully made.

Wonderful are your works;

my soul knows it very well.

My frame was not hidden from you,

when I was being made in the secret,

intricately woven in the depths of the earth.

Your eyes saw my unformed substance;

in your book were written, every one of them,

the days that were formed for me,

when as yet there was none of them.

David writes these Bible verses almost as if he were writing a personal letter to someone he refers to as "you." Who do you think the words "you" and "your" refer to? Write your answer in the space below.

The answer is God. God created David (and you and me), and in this passage we read a lot of words that describe *how* he created us! What kinds of verbs, or action words, describe how God made David? Grab your purple marker and circle any verbs in the passage above that answer that question.

Now, fill in the blanks below by writing what God did to create you.

1._____   **2.**_____

3. _____

Are those three things accidental or intentional? Circle your choice with your favorite color.

So, based on what you're reading, circle the sentence below that God would have been most likely to say when you were born:

"WHOOPS! I MADE A GIRL?"
OR
"THERE SHE IS—THE MASTERPIECE
I HAD PLANNED ALL ALONG!"

We vote strongly that he said, "There she is—the masterpiece I had planned all along!" How do we know this? Because no one ever weaves, knits, or forms something without carefully laying out a plan. All of these actions require planning. Weaving and knitting even require math! God *planned* you. *Formed* your body. *Wove* you together. And *knit* you into a masterpiece.

Using all the markers you have, in the box below draw a picture of a weaving that would represent you. Use your favorite colors. Make your favorite shapes or symbols. Be creative.

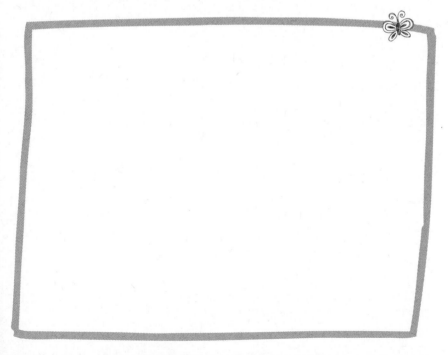

SKG
Puzzle Craze

The Uses of Your Body

Your body might seem to be made for clothes or exercise or eating or feeding, but God's purposes for it are so much more important. Look up each of the Bible verses below and discover what your body is in God's eyes.

CLUES

Each word speaks of something that your body is for God.
(*Big hint: Like the word "vessel."*)

ACROSS
3. 1 Corinthians 3:16-17

DOWN
1. 1 Peter 2:5
2. Ephesians 2:19-22

For puzzle answers go to page 118.

Look Inside Yourself

After you "DIG IN" by becoming a studier of the Bible, it's time to get ready to become a pray-er. We like to start by looking inside our own hearts before we talk to God. This is like a bridge between studying and praying. When you see the "Look Inside" symbol, it means I'm getting ready to ask you some super-personal questions. Ready?

1 Select one from each pair by putting a check mark by each thing you believe about your body. I am (or I feel as if I am)…

_____ Wonderfully made   _____ Imperfectly crafted

_____ Seen and known by God   _____ Alone and afraid

_____ A house fit for God   _____ Unworthy of being God's home

2 Fill in the blank, selecting one of the areas above where you hope God can change you.

I wish I were more _____.

3 Based on what you learned today in our practice meditation about your body, do you believe what you want to about your body, or do you believe what God says about your body? Circle one.

♥ I think I believe what God says about my body.

♥ I seem more influenced by what the world says about my body than what God says.

♥ I'm a little confused and need to keep studying and praying.

4 What do you think you need to do based on what you've just studied while "digging in"?

Reach Up to Talk to GOD

When you see this graphic,

you're going to add praying to your studying. I (Dannah) like to write my prayers down in a journal or diary. To help you learn how to do that, Suzy and I are going to help you write your prayers to God based on what we've just studied. **First, fill in the blanks to personalize your prayer. Then pray your prayer out loud.**

Dear _____ (your favorite name for God),

You are so_____ (your favorite descriptive word for God)! I praise you for who you are and for creating me and my body! I want to believe what you say about my body and its worth. Please help me, especially in the area of _____. I am really struggling in this area and this makes me feel _____.

Will you help me? As I start this Secret Keeper Girl Bible study, I promise to meditate by studying the Bible and then praying. I look forward to what you'll do in me to change me. I'm feeling very… _____ excited _____ overwhelmed.

I give this emotion to you.
In Jesus' name,

_____

(sign here)

Congratulations! You just meditated. Now that you've practiced, we're ready to meditate on God's truth about your body. Welcome to *It's Great to Be a Girl!*

Your Body, a Purpose

You were bought with a price.
So glorify God in your body.
1 CORINTHIANS 6:20

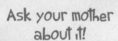

Ask your mother about it!

The first time I (Suzy) went scuba diving, I experienced a horrible fright. I saw a barracuda that was more than six feet long, but I didn't know what a barracuda was (it's only one of the most dangerous predators in the ocean—no big deal), so that was not my trauma. No, my panic occurred when I cut myself on a sharp piece of coral, and black liquid started gushing from my kneecap. *Black!* My mind immediately went into worst-case scenario mode. *That coral was poisonous, and it's given me some sort of rare blood disease that made my blood turn black! This is not good! I have to get to the surface. I have to get to the hospital!*

My scuba instructor saw my frantic gestures and graciously swam 40 feet to the surface with me. Imagine my confusion when I told him my story and shared my concern...and he laughed!

"You scraped your knee," he told me. "Forty feet down, there aren't many red wavelengths from sunlight visible, so red appears to be black. Look at your knee now." Sure enough, there it was, oozing little jets of red into the cool blue Caribbean. He still made me get out of the water. Apparently blood is a little too tempting for barracuda.

The first time I got my period was just as wacky and frightening. I guess I hadn't talked to my mom very much about it. I think I was in seventh grade. I know I was at school. It wasn't much. I was able to fold up some toilet paper in my underwear, and that did the trick, even through track practice. I waited two days (until toilet paper wasn't enough) before I sheepishly told my mom and asked her what to do.

"Honey, why did you wait to tell me?" she asked.

I gave her the classic answer—"I don't know."

If I could give you a piece of advice about learning about your body it would be this: Don't wait. Talk now. Talk early and talk often.

What does "talk often" mean? It means this is not a taboo topic of conversation. None of the topics in this book are off-limits. In fact, once you get comfortable with them, they're the kind of things you include in everyday conversations. Every girl gets a period. Every girl needs deodorant so her armpits don't create a stench that would kill Bigfoot. Every girl wonders if she is ready to shave. And every girl eventually has to go bra shopping. There, see? I brought that

BODY HOMEWORK

Instead of telling you everything about growing up, we're just going to give you a few key ideas and let you talk through the details with your mom or another woman who has stepped up in your life to be like a mom to you. We highly recommend you use this book along with *Raising Body-Confident Daughters* by Dannah. But even if you're not including those dates, here's today's homework. Pick the topic we just mentioned that most terrifies you—bras, deodorant, shaving, or periods—and go ask your mom about it! Trust us. She'll be honored if you bring your questions to her.

one out in the open too! These are all things girls can talk about without being embarrassed. They're common. They're ordinary. And they're normal parts of this adventure that Dannah and I are going to guide you through called puberty.

What are we waiting for? **Let's start talking!**

THREE FACTS ABOUT PUBERTY EVERY GIRL MUST KNOW

FACT 1: It's hard to know when you've officially started the period of life called puberty.

No one hands out certificates or anything, and every girl develops at a different rate. Many girls *start* puberty by their tenth birthday. But some girls get started as early as eight years old, and others might be twelve or thirteen when they begin. There are a lot of factors that determine when

you will begin to grow breasts and when you will have your first period. Our genes play a role, as do the things we eat, the amount of physical activity we engage in, and even our race—black girls tend to mature a little faster than Asian girls or white girls. One of the earliest signs is usually breast buds—a noticeable swelling that will require your first bra. Around the same time you notice these breast buds, you may notice the growth of dark hair in new places—under your arms, on your legs… and when you go to the bathroom, you may also notice the appearance of pubic hair. Even before breast buds appear, you may notice the need to begin using deodorant (we're talking body odor, ladies!) and some acne on your face or arms. Of course, the major landmark in this journey will be your first period. (More on many of these big events later in the book!)

FACT 2: All the changes in your body are happening for a reason.

God has arranged all that is necessary for your body to be fully ready to make babies one day—from increased body fat so you can safely carry a baby inside of you someday, to breasts for feeding a baby. A girl is not supposed to be perfectly lean and tight like a boy might expect to be, even if fashion magazines suggest otherwise. Our bodies were meant to have curves and some extra body fat to provide nutrients for the life that God may one day knit together inside our womb. We need breasts to feed a newborn the healthiest and most important nutrients. Everything else you're going through during puberty is preparing your body to be a glorious, beautiful vessel of life. God is getting you ready to be a mom!

FACT 3: Changes to our bodies can be crazy scary or uncomfortable, but they're completely normal and safe.

Some people say the only person who likes change is a baby in a wet diaper! We get comfortable with our normal life. Change is scary because we have no idea what it will bring. If you feel a little nervous about your body changing, don't worry. We have already been on the journey, and we're here to tell you it may be a little uncomfortable and embarrassing at times, but it's all for the good. Do you know what we've found embarrassment and discomfort to be good for? Bonding! We (Dannah and Suzy) grow closer as friends when we go through something uncomfortable together. It gives us great fits of laughter! Have you and your mom ever laughed so hard together that you've both cried? Nothing like a good awkward moment for making memories.

pu•ber•ty
(noun) • : *the period of life when a person's sexual organs mature and she becomes able to have children*

All right—ready to get to the homework? Make a date with your mom or your go-to advice-giving woman! It can be a pizza date, an ice-cream date, a nail painting date, a fancy dinner date… any of those will do. Try to find a private, comfortable setting where you won't be interrupted and you don't feel like you need to speak in hushed whispers. And then talk.

 **THINK ABOUT IT**

Use this box to create a list of questions you do NOT want to forget to ask!

meditation 1

Your Body, a Purpose

W e're about to tell you something really big! It may be good news to you, or it may be bad news. Here goes: Women were not created for the sole purpose of having babies. Even though puberty is all about getting your body ready to do just that, God has a much bigger purpose in mind for your body.

Maybe you just breathed a sigh of relief because having a baby is one of the last things on your mind right now. (Give it a few years, friend.) Maybe you feel confused about that statement because you have been hoping to be a mom since you picked up your first baby doll. No matter how you feel about it, we're going to start this book off with the truth about why God created you to be a woman.

Yes, women are built to make babies. Yes, God did give Adam and Eve (and everyone born since then) a command to populate the earth by having children. And yes, having kids is a blessing. But it is not the *purpose* for your existence. It's a good thing, too, because a lot of women are not able to have children for one reason or another. I (Suzy) am one of them, but I became a mom through adoption. And those of us who cannot or do not make babies need to know that God loves us every bit as much as he loves other women! Let's dig in deep to find out what God really intended when he created these bodies of ours.

DIG IN by Studying Luke 2:1-20

You're probably familiar with the events of Christmas, but did you know that this story also tells us about the purpose of our bodies? Read the story below. The shepherds were the first ones in the Christmas story to figure out their purpose.

Find the song the angels sang to them below and circle the word "glory" with a bright yellow marker. See if you can find that word or a form of it anywhere else in the passage. *(Hint: You will find one more use of that word.)*

1 In those days a decree went out from Caesar Augustus that all the world should be registered. **2** This was the first registration when Quirinius was governor of Syria. **3** And all went to be registered, each to his own town. **4** And Joseph also went up from Galilee, from the town of Nazareth, to Judea, to the city of David, which is called Bethlehem, because he was of the house and lineage of David, **5** to be registered with Mary, his betrothed, who was with child. **6** And while they were there, the time came for her to give birth. **7** And she gave birth to her firstborn son and wrapped him in swaddling cloths and laid him in a manger, because there was no place for them in the inn. **8** And in the same region there were shepherds out in the field, keeping watch over their flock by night. **9** And an angel of the Lord appeared to them, and the glory of the Lord shone around them, and they were filled with great fear. **10** And the angel said to them, "Fear not, for behold, I bring you good news of great joy that will be for all the people. **11** For unto you is born this day in the city of David a Savior, who is Christ the Lord. **12** And this

will be a sign for you: you will find a baby wrapped in swaddling cloths

and lying in a manger." **13** And suddenly there was with the angel a

multitude of the heavenly host praising God and saying,

14 "Glory to God in the highest, and on earth

peace among those with whom he is pleased!"

15 When the angels went away from them into heaven, the shepherds

said to one another, "Let us go over to Bethlehem and see this thing

that has happened, which the Lord has made known to us."

16 And they went with haste and found Mary and Joseph, and the

baby lying in a manger. **17** And when they saw it, they made known

the saying that had been told them concerning this child. **18** And all

who heard it wondered at what the shepherds told them.

19 But Mary treasured up all these things, pondering them in

her heart. **20** And the shepherds returned, glorifying and

praising God for all they had heard and seen, as it had

been told them (Luke 2:1-20).

SKG
Puzzle Craze

Use the word bank below to fill in the blanks in this paragraph.

JESUS   MARY   PREGNANT   SHEPHERDS   HOLY

BETHLEHEM   HOMETOWN   GLORIFYING   JOSEPH

ROOM   MANGER   ANGELS   GLORY

Mary was a virgin and not married yet to _____.

God used _____ to create Jesus' body, but he did not use

Joseph; Mary became _____ by a miracle of God's

_____ Spirit. Jesus was born in _____,

which was not his parents' _____. Because there

was no _____ for the family anywhere in town, _____

was born and laid in a _____. _____

informed the _____ of the birth by saying, "_____

to God in the highest." The shepherds were fast learners because

pretty soon they were _____ God.

For puzzle answers go to page 118.

What did the angels teach the shepherds to do?

_____ GOD!

[What's our purpose? God created us to
glorify him. That's our number one job.]

To glorify God means to make him visible or known—sort of the way the moon makes the sun known. The moon has no light of its own, but it can be seen as it reflects the light of the sun. In this way the moon "glorifies" the sun. God is like the sun, and we are meant to be like the moon.

Circle the specific thing we are supposed to use when we glorify or make God known.

> 66 You were bought with a price.
> So glorify God in your body
> (1 Corinthians 6:20).

Specifically what part of us is supposed to glorify him?

Our _____.

Our bodies are created and exist to glorify God. One way—but not the only way—we women do this is through childbirth. Interestingly, God's Son didn't appear out of thin air when he came to save us. He arrived like every other person—through birth. And for this reason, he created all women with the ability to bear new life! Making babies is an important way God has glorified himself through women. Every great doctor, theologian, prayer warrior, or poet who has ever lived spent the first nine months of his or her life in a warm, safe womb (and the next nine months spitting up and needing diaper changes!). But people have never been and will never be the superstars in this story of life. God has always been and will always be the famous one. Our job is to make his fame more and more known *with our bodies.*

Look Inside Yourself

We don't have babies often. That is a rare and precious occurrence in life. (Dannah has given birth twice and also has one child who was adopted. Suzy has never given birth but has two children who were adopted.) Do we glorify God with our bodies *only* when we give birth? Nope. There's so much more to it.

Circle the two actions we do with our bodies that are specifically named in this verse.

 So, whether you eat or drink, or whatever you do, do it all for the glory of God (1 Corinthians 10:31).

Eating and drinking with our bodies can glorify God. But so can "whatever you do." We can glorify God when we are bathing, painting our toes, doing gymnastics, watching television, or singing songs. What kinds of things do you like to do with your body? Use your markers to doodle, draw pictures of, or write out as many things as you can possibly think of in the squares below that you can do with your body. (Keep in mind that *everything* you write down can be for his glory.)

Reach Up to Talk to GOD

Dear Jesus,

Wow. This is deep stuff. I see that the purpose of my body is to _____ God. Help me to eat and drink to _____ you. Today I also thought of these things that I do with my body, and I hope you'll help me do them to your glory. They include _____, _____, _____, and _____.

Thank you for showing me my purpose in your plan. Forgive me for times when I've tried to be the famous one. I know my main purpose on Earth is to shine light on you. In everything I do, help me to point people straight to you. You alone are the famous one!

All my love,

_____

(sign here)

Your Body, Its Practice

So God created man in his own image, in the image of God
he created him; male and female he created them.

GENESIS 1:27

Ugh! My Hair!

Right now I (Suzy) am out on the Secret Keeper Girl Tour, living in our big, black tour bus, as I often am, and the weather is wet and humid. If you have curly hair like mine —I mean really curly and thick—this translates to only one thing. Today is afro day. But it's not a cute afro. It's round and frizzy and…ugh!

I definitely did not get my mom's hair. My mom's hair is straight and thin, and I have always wanted straight, thin hair. Nope, I got my dad's hair— curly and thick. (I guess I should be really grateful that my thick, curly hair hasn't fallen out like his did!) I did get my mom's skin though. It's a little dry, so it needs help from moisturizer, but I'm thankful for her clear complexion. She and I rarely need or wear makeup. To this day I don't wear anything other than moisturizer or cover up, just like my mom.

I wonder if I would wear a lot of makeup if she had? In so many ways, I'm an image of my mom and my dad.

Ugh! My Hair!

Right now I (Dannah) am sitting in Secret Keeper Girl headquarters. My office is cozy and cute with a bright needlepoint ottoman in the middle of it, which is just what I need on rainy days like this one. If you have hair like mine—straight and thin—this translates into only one thing. Today is afro day. My hair isn't super short, so it's long, rebellious afro day. I look very much like I'm about to begin growing dreadlocks. (Ask your big sister or mom what those are if you don't know.)

im•age

(noun) • : *a physical likeness or representation of a person, animal, or thing, photographed, painted, sculptured, or otherwise made visible.*

I got my mom's hair. It's thin and straight—though the wheat-like color came from my dad. I also got her oily skin, which I'm told is a blessing because I'll wrinkle less, but it means I wear makeup *to cover up the zits*! I wonder if I wear makeup because she does? In so many ways, I'm an image of my mom and dad.

Same Problem. Different Hair.

We believe it's not the hair, but the heart that makes us happy or sad with our appearance. And we also believe that it's really important for you start getting happy with how you look because you are a carefully crafted masterpiece.

Today we're going to take a look in the mirror and try to figure out who you look like. You might look like your mom or dad, but you were created to look like God too!

Here we go!

MADE UP

This might be a good place to talk about the fun subject of makeup. Every girl has fun with a little lip gloss now and then. When are you old enough to start wearing it? Our answer is actually a question: What is your motivation? Here are three reasons you might want to wear makeup—and what we think of them.

Reason 1: Makeup = Cover-Up

Lots of people wear makeup to cover up scars, acne, or birthmarks. I (Dannah) began to wear a very light foundation in seventh grade for this very reason. Some light foundation might be a blessing, but be careful not to overuse it. This can lead to both more clogging of your pores (which means more zits) and a comical look as you actually begin accentuating the blemishes instead of hiding them. The Bible says everything should be done in moderation, and that can certainly apply to makeup! So reason number one is a good one if done with moderation!

makeup is fun to talk about!

Reason 2: Makeup = Beauty

Who says makeup makes a person beautiful? Perhaps you've heard this famous saying: Beauty is in the eye of the beholder. That means everyone has her own definition of what is pleasing to look at. There is no true-or-false standard when it comes to beauty. So does makeup make a girl more beautiful? That depends on those who are looking at the girl. Most of the time, people agree that too much makeup takes away from a person's beauty instead of adding to it. So reason number two is not true at all.

Reason 3: Makeup = Maturity

When we wear makeup to make people think we are older than we actually are, have we kind of told a lie? We think so. Lies are anything we say or fail to say (or anything we do or fail to do) that causes others to have an impression that's not true. Enjoy your youth. So regarding reason number three, it's best to look your age.

When should you begin to wear makeup? That can be tough to figure out. (Suzy still wears it only on stage. But that's just a preference.)
Here's our answer...

💜 when Mom and Dad say it's okay

💜 when the reason for wearing it isn't to trick others into thinking you are older than you really are

💜 when you can honestly say you are okay without it

💜 when there is a blemish (maybe a pimple) that you want to cover up

💜 when you know you are God's masterpiece even without a makeup brush in your hand

Then you're ready.

 **THINK ABOUT IT**

What would be YOUR motivation for wearing make up?

_____

_____

_____

_____

meditation 2

Your Body, Its Practice

Sometimes when I (Dannah) am doing my Beth Moore Bible study, I learn something so thrilling that I just have to tell someone. I run around all day as if the world is my classroom, explaining step-by-step how God taught me something new that morning. I know I'm not alone because sometimes I see Suzy posting a Bible verse or sentence of truth on her Twitter or Instagram page. She's found something thrilling and is bursting to tell someone, so she does. I know how it feels—as if I simply must get out a megaphone to cheer for God and the lessons he gives. I can't help it when he's blown my mind!

Prepare to have your mind blown today! I'm praying that today you will just *have* to tell someone what you've discovered from God. What we're going to learn in this meditation is something that some people who have been Christians for decades have never heard. It's one of the biggest secrets to the Christian life, and yet God never wanted it to be a secret at all. In fact, it's time to get out *your* megaphone and start to shout this one out. But first we've got to learn it so we can embrace it with our whole being!

We're going to start a bit backward today, saving the Bible verses for later. Let's start by taking a good look at *you.*

Look Inside Yourself

Determine whose image you bear.

An image is a picture, statue, or likeness of someone else. Whose image do you bear? That is to say, who do you look like? Your mom? Your dad? Your great-grandma from Tokyo? Your uncle from Alaska? Sometimes we figure this out best by taking it piece-by-piece. Grab a mirror and look at each part of yourself carefully. When you've decided who you look like in a certain area, write their name in the space provided. If you have trouble figuring one out, ask for help from someone who knows you and your family well.

My EYES look like _____.

My NOSE looks like _____.

My BODY TYPE takes after _____.

The SHAPE OF MY HEAD matches _____.

I have my _____'s HAIR.

And my _____'s HANDS.

People say I WALK like _____.

And I TALK like _____.

That exercise wasn't easy if you've been adopted. In fact, it could make you sort of sad if you don't know what your biological mom and dad look like. We understand! As mothers of three adopted girls, we're super sensitive about the fact that they wonder who they look like. But Autumn belongs to Dannah. And Rachael and Marie belong to Suzy. As a result we spend a lot of time together. Our adopted girls have picked up some of our habits and mannerisms. Sometime I (Dannah) like to find ways that Autumn is like me. For example, we both like to get things done early in the day. We're both super organized and like our bedrooms clean. Finding these commonalities takes away the sting of not looking alike. Maybe you could try that. In fact, let's all try it, adopted or not.

Write a list of ways that you have become like your mom and/or dad in the space below. Maybe you both say the same phrase or sentence a lot. Maybe you both love ice cream or baseball. Pick as many things about you that have been influenced by your parents as you can think of.

BONUS!
Look
Inside
Yourself

Chosen Image: Write down some ways that you act like your mom or dad. Sometimes we are around people we live with and love so much that we become like them in the way we act.

DIG IN by Studying Genesis 1:26-31; 2 Corinthians 3:18

We turn again to another very familiar story from the Bible—creation. No doubt you've heard this familiar phrase: "In the beginning, God created." This is where we find out just how God planned for us to bring him glory. Remember that word from your last meditation? Write what it means by filling in the blanks below. (If you need help, turn back to page 27.)

To glorify God means to make him

_____ or_____.[27]

Today we're going to learn that he had this in mind all along—from the very point of creation. Way back then he was thinking of what you would look like. Yep, it has a lot to do with your image. Use a bright yellow marker to circle the word "image" or any word that is like "image" (Hint: "likeness") when you find it below.

26 Then God said, "Let us make man in our image,

after our likeness. And let them have dominion over the fish of the sea

and over the birds of the heavens and over the livestock and over all

the earth and over every creeping thing that creeps on the earth."

27 *So God created man in his own image, in the image of God*

he created him; male and female he created them.

28 And God blessed them. And God said to them, "Be fruitful and

multiply and fill the earth and subdue it, and have dominion over the fish of the sea and over the birds of the heavens and over

every living thing that moves on the earth." **29** And God said,

"Behold, I have given you every plant yielding seed that is on the face

of all the earth, and every tree with seed in its fruit. You shall have them

for food. **30** And to every beast of the earth and to every bird of the

heavens and to everything that creeps on the earth, everything that

has the breath of life, I have given every green plant for food."

And it was so. **31** And God saw everything that he had made,

and behold, it was very good. And there was evening and there was

morning, the sixth day (Genesis 1:26-31).

According to the passage above, you weren't created in the image of your mother, the image of your father, or the image of your grandparents, regardless of whose nose you might sport on the front of your face. You were created in the image of God, and he has an opinion about that. Let's see what it is. Draw a bunch of big arrows pointing to the word in verse 31 that completes this sentence. Then fill in the blank below.

"And God saw everything that he had made,

and behold, it was very _____."

God says that the fact that you are made in his image is very *good*! It might be because we make God visible or known (we glorify him) by looking like him! How cool is that? And it gets even cooler!

Grab a couple markers and use them to circle the words "male" and "female." (Use your favorite color to circle "female!" It doesn't have to be the stereotypical "girlie" pink, mind you!) Now answer this question by filling in the two blanks:

What two things does Genesis 1:27 specifically mention when it says that humans are created in the image of God?

1. _____ **2.** _____

God specifically points out that our biological sex is a trait that makes us look like him. There are lots of things that make us like God. Our brains. Our creativity. But God mentions only maleness and femaleness in Genesis when he says we are created in his image. It seems like being a girl is a BIG DEAL! (And so is being a boy!) Any ideas on WHY he chose two very distinctly different sexes to represent him?

That's a super hard question, so we're going to help you. It's because God is three distinctly different persons, all in one being. He is God the Father, God the Son, and God the Holy Spirit. He is three distinct persons and yet one being—the Trinity. The Hebrew word in the Bible for this unity is *echad*.

One male and one female are capable of being united by God into marriage. God created male and female to be distinctly different but capable of being united into one. The Hebrew word in the Bible for this unity is also *echad*. Just look at this Bible verse:

This is why a man leaves his father and mother and is united to his wife, and they become one [echad] flesh (Genesis 2:24 NIV).

The male and the female are two distinct, independent humans, but when they come together, they are *echad*. An ancient Jewish prayer cries out, "Hear, O Israel: The LORD our God, the LORD is one [*echad*]" (Deuteronomy 6:4).

If our purpose is to glorify God, our practice—the act that makes our purpose possible—is to embrace his image in us by being girls.

> [What's our practice? God created us as females to reflect his image. That's how we glorify him best.]

This is super heavy-duty brain food, but we think you're capable of handling it all. Let's look at one more Bible verse while we're digging in. Use your yellow marker again and circle the word "image."

> 66 And we all, with unveiled face, beholding the glory of the Lord, are being transformed into the same image from one degree of glory to another. For this comes from the Lord who is the Spirit (2 Corinthians 3:18).

Using your yellow marker, underline the verb phrase (it's two words long) that shows up just a few words before the word "image."

You should have underlined "being transformed." What does this say about the fact that we are made in God's image? Write about it below.

 _____

_____

_____

_____

We are *still* being made to look more and more like him. Through Christ you will always be in the process of becoming the image of God. He transforms us continually into being what makes us most like him and most capable of glorifying him. He starts with the fact that you are a girl, and he continues working in you from there!

SKG
Puzzle Craze

Find these important words in the word search below. As you do, remember what they mean and how they fit into your purpose to glorify God.

ECHAD   FEMALE   IMAGE   MALE   TRANSFORMED

E G D C W G B E V K N B S N D

D X E M Y Y L X R F W K B A B

Y K M M S A E Z T P T U P K Q

L A R J M E R H C S C B V O S

Y B O E Y R B Z I H C M D G N

R J F E Y A X L X D P B U H D

D B S J N E P X L Z Q S N Q M

D T N T V I J O Z E E S X P U

S V A O Y H M F H J J D D I D

A C R S D U P A X F Z C I A H

F E T H K L C B G Y M M K I U

F O V O K T D J G E A T X W H

E C H A D C R N U L L K D Z I

T L Y U K L L X M L E F T N N

J K P M B P N V N Z G X G L I

For puzzle answers go to page 118.

Look Inside Yourself

Embrace whose image you bear. This lesson is so important that we're going to let you take a second look inside your heart. This time we want to ask you this question: Can you accept and embrace the One whose image you bear?

As we shared at the beginning of this chapter, sometimes we complain about our hair! And sometimes we complain about our skin or other parts of our bodies too. As girls, we don't often like how we look. In this way, we reject our mom's eyes, or our dad's hair, or our grandma's long, crooked, pointy finger. (Dannah got that from her dad's mom.) Is that okay? We don't think it is. It's rejecting what God created. And in the passage you just studied, God says that what he created is **good**! You should believe that your nose, hair, eyes, and body are good.

Let's take this one step farther. You are also supposed to believe that being made in God's image is *good*. The fact that you are female and able to fulfill your purpose to glorify God as a girl is something you should embrace. Some people reject it, probably because they don't understand God's good purpose and plan. Or maybe they're just confused.

[You are a girl. That glorifies God. It is good. **]**

It doesn't matter if you are a hunting, football-loving, blue-wearing girl or a painting, gymnastics-loving, pink-wearing girl. God chose for you to be a girl.

 **THINK ABOUT IT**

What kind of girl are you, and will you choose to embrace being a girl no matter how unique you are?

Reach Up to Talk to GOD

Dear Jesus,

Here I am. A girl. Being a girl makes me feel _____

_____.

I did / didn't (**circle one**) know how important being a girl was, but now I have studied about it and realize more than ever that it is what helps other people to recognize you. It is how we glorify you. Here are some questions on my heart about being a girl.

1. _____

_____

2. _____

_____

3. _____

_____

I want to look like you so others can see you in me. Keep transforming me. I know that what you have created in me is *good*!

In Jesus' name,
AMEN!

Your Body, God's Temple

*Do you not know that you are God's
temple and that God's Spirit dwells in you?
If anyone destroys God's temple, God will
destroy him. For God's temple is holy,
and you are that temple.*
1 CORINTHIANS 3:16-17

We love our puppies. Between the two of us, we have three. Moose, the chocolate labradoodle, belongs to Dannah. Biscuit, the golden retriever, and Hero, the Bernese Mountain dog, belong to Suzy. We are just NUTS about our dogs, and we'd probably love yours too. We know it's a tad soon to start doling out assignments, but draw a picture of your dog on the next page and include his or her name and breed. (If you don't have a dog, you can draw a photo of your cat. We love them too. We have four between the two of us.)

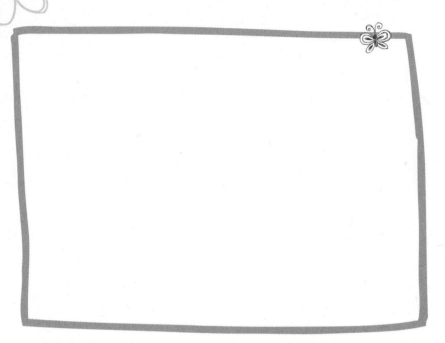

PAWS TO CONSIDER THE COST

Dogs need food, toys, beds, doctor visits, leashes, medicine, grooming, occasional dogsitting…so the average dog owner will spend between $1000 and $3000 each year on a dog. Over the course of a ten-year life span, that's $10,000—$30,000 per dog!

As your parents may have pointed out to you, raising dogs and caring for them costs money. A LOT of money! And when it's time to go away from home, you can't… until you find some other dog-crazy person who will help you with your beloved four-footed critter. When we go away, we ask people to take care of our dogs, and it doesn't always go so well. I (Suzy) had a bad experience once when we asked a friend to stay with our Dalmatians. I don't know if our friend was too busy or afraid of muddy doggy paws, but for a full week the dogs were put in the backyard and then ushered immediately into our basement. (Oh, those dogs must have hated that! We tend to be those dog-in-the-bed types.) When we arrived home, we found a full week's worth of dried mud as well as fat, well-fed ticks on our beloved fur babies. Not. Good. That was the moment we realized no one was likely to take care of our dogs the way we would.

Guess what? No one is going to take care of *you* quite the way you do either. And by now you have probably also realized that the human body, especially the body about to hit puberty, needs way more care than a puppy dog does.

There are several places where the Bible tells us to take care of our bodies and gives reasons as well. Today we'll look at what God says about your body and begin learning about important things like bathing, shaving, deodorant, and cleansing your face! Just as you have to learn to cook or play an instrument, you'll have to learn some skills in order to care for your body, so...let's go to school.

BODY BOOSTS
Body Boost 1: SOAP

Boys aren't the only ones who are stinky. You'll just have to trust us because we aren't always the best judges of what we smell like. Let's make sure the smells we are broadcasting to the world cooperate with our desire to have others near us by committing to **daily or every-other day bubble baths or showers.** You can do this in the morning or at night if that fits your schedule better, but it's time to get serious about it.

Body Boost 2: FACIAL CLEANSER

So what causes pimples, or acne? It's pretty complicated because God's design of your body is crazy good. Your skin is full of pores (or hair follicles) that produce their own oils. The oil-producing glands in your pores are called sebaceous glands. Puberty hormones tell these sebaceous glands to increase production of skin oil, but sometimes the glands work a little overtime, and dead skin cells or bacteria get trapped inside our pores along with too much oil. This produces a pimple.

Two things prevent pimples—keeping your face clean and keeping your hands clean (especially before you cleanse or touch your face). You can really prevent them by starting to wash your face regularly *before* they start to show up!

pimples are crazy!

Once one shows up, it's best to let it run its natural course. It'll most likely be gone within a week. If the pimple does turn white, that means the trapped oils and bacteria are near the surface and can be more safely "popped," though you should never deal with pimples unless your hands are washed and you are able to immediately put an antibacterial wash on the sore. If you can, resist the temptation to pop a pimple. Makeup is a great and safe way to cover the redness. (Remember to use it moderately!)

Best way to prevent pimples to begin with? **Wash your face every morning and night like clockwork,** but there's no need to wash too often or to scrub like crazy. Again, God's design is amazing. A simple wash will remove dead skin cells, which are the main culprits getting trapped in those open pores. If you use a moisturizing cream afterward, be sure it is "non-acnegenic"—a fancy way to say it does not clog your pores. And watch out for those hair sprays and gels! They tend to make acne worse.

Body Boost 3: DEODORANT

Time to start using deodorant every day. There are very few things as offensive to other people's noses as body odor. But we're willing to bet your own nose has taught you that already. You might be one of the few lucky ones who don't need to wear deodorant every day. Want to hear a simple rule that applies to much of life? Less is more. It can't get much easier than that, can it? Less deodorant. Less perfume. Less offending other people even with your good smells. It can be tempting to put on a lot of something that smells really good. But a lot of perfume…well, it smells really bad.

Body Boost 4: RAZOR

Eventually you'll most likely want to shave your legs and underneath your arms. Shaving is one of the more difficult hygiene practices to master. No one is good at this one right from the start, which is a bit of a scary thought since we're talking about a sharp object! There is no rush to begin, but once you do begin you'll need to **shave at least once a week** to keep your hair trimmed and soft, so don't start until you're comfortable with that commitment.

There are alternatives to shaving, though none are as quick or as cheap. One alternative is waxing, which is just what it sounds like. Hot wax (not so hot it burns) is applied to the skin, and a strip of paper or cloth is applied to the waxy skin. After a second of warmth, the strip is ripped from the skin, taking the wax and the hair (from the root) with it. OUCH! Why wax? The hair stays gone longer. A lot longer. Why not wax? Pain would be a good reason number one, along with the fact that waxing has a tendency to cause pimples. It's also a lot more expensive than a razor and soap.

Body Boost 5: WATER

Did you know that drinking water will make you beautiful? It's true. Of course, it's also important for other reasons. Water helps you digest food and circulate blood, and it even makes it easier to…um…"excrete." But drinking water will help you have healthier-looking, glowing skin. After all, your skin is an organ made up of cells, and cells are made up of water. They need water to function well. If you don't drink enough water, your skin could become dry and itchy.

There are two ways to care for your body with water. One is to drink it! Lots of it. **Your goal should be to drink an eight-ounce glass of water eight times a day**. Having a water bottle with ounces marked on it will help you remember how much to drink. A second way is to **moisturize within two minutes of leaving the bath or shower**. This sort of seals the water into your pores so you stay hydrated. Just slather on some good moisturizer.

meditation 3

Your Body, God's Temple

Both of my (Suzy's) daughters were adopted as teenagers. I wish so much that I could have known them when they were young, but instead I only have the stories they tell. When Marie was about 15 we took her to see a movie called *The Blind Side*—the story of an enormous black teenager from the South who was adopted by a white family. The mom, played by Sandra Bullock, used food and comfort—including his very first bed—to make him feel loved, and they used football to motivate him to study. He went on to become an NFL player. Though his life was clearly different from my 110-pound, non-football-playing, stylish white girl from Santa Barbara, California, she felt as if their lives were very similar.

As we walked out of the movie, she said quietly, "I never had my own bed either." Just like the football player, Marie had spent years of her life moving from place to place, wearing secondhand clothes, having uncombed hair on school picture day...and until she was 14 she never had a bed to call her own. No one ever walked her through "hygiene school" the way we're walking with you right now.

Let me be honest—as Marie and I talked about this chapter, she has been worried about you. She was concerned because you might not have had anyone talk to you about being clean. She wanted you to know that being clean is not a standard of godliness. In fact, hygiene isn't even mentioned in the Bible.

SKG
Puzzle Craze

Unscramble this popular saying using the words below. They are in the correct order. All you have to do is unscramble the words.

enelCasnils _____

si _____ netx _____ ot_____

osedgslin _____

Write the sentence out below.

_____   _____   _____

_____   _____.

Do you think that's a Bible verse? It sure sounds like one, but it's not. The Bible never says being clean on the outside makes you more like God. But the misunderstanding is an honest one. Here's why.

First, the Old Testament refers to people being clean or unclean. But those words didn't mean what they mean to us today. People who were able to participate in Jewish worship rituals and community life were called clean. People who were disqualified for some reason were called unclean.

Many of the first Jews who followed Jesus believed that people who became Christians should continue following a lot of those Old Testament rituals that had formerly made people acceptable to God. However, followers of Jesus were given tremendous freedom because they learned that rituals could never cleanse people's hearts—only Jesus can do that! When we ask Christ to dwell inside of us, he makes our hearts clean.

His death on the cross makes all this possible (more on this straight ahead). Embracing this truth is what makes us Christians. If you have never asked Jesus to be the Lord of your life and cleanse you on the inside, turn to the end of this chapter and read "The ABCs of Becoming a Christian" right now.

DIG IN by Studying 1 Corinthians 3:16-17; 10:24; 3 John 1:2

As we look at the entire Bible, it seems there are three reasons to be clean. Let's look at each of them by studying a few passages. We're going to let you fill in the blanks, so pay close attention!

 Do you not know that you are God's temple

and that God's Spirit dwells in you? If anyone destroys God's temple,

God will destroy him. For God's temple is holy, and you are

that temple (1 Corinthians 3:16-17).

The passage above reads,

"You are _____ _____."

Use your red marker to circle what you are. Then circle every time it shows up in those verses.

A temple is a place where God lives. If you have asked Christ to be Lord of your life, his Spirit lives inside of you. *You are God's temple.* Obviously, you want to take care of God's house, don't you? The first reason to take care of your body is that it is *God's temple.* Write that in the space below.

REASON 1: _____

Let no one seek his own good, but the good of his neighbor (1 Corinthians 10:24).

Using the verse above, fill in the blanks.

No one _____ seek their own _____,

but the good of _____.

Being clean on the outside, as much as we are able, is kind of important for being close to other people. The second reason we should stay clean is the comfort of other people. We are supposed to look like God so we can help other people meet him (remember our last meditation?). By smelling good and presenting ourselves well, we can make sure they are comfortable around us. *The comfort of others* is the second reason to be clean. Write that in the space below.

REASON 2: _____

Beloved, I pray that all may go well with you and that you may be in good health, as it goes well with your soul (3 John 2).

Circle the words "good health."

God wants you to be healthy, and being clean promotes good health. Some of the Old Testament laws contain very practical advice about hygiene. God told the Israelites not to touch dead bodies, which can carry disease. He told them to make soap because being clean protects us from disease. God wants us to be well. He wants us to be useful.

hy•giene

(noun) • : conditions or practices related to taking care of your body and health, especially related to cleanliness

I (Suzy) recently started running. I have been in a couple of races, and it's starting to get fun. I have dropped a couple of pant sizes, and I won't pretend that hasn't felt good too. But that wasn't the main reason I began. I have met some fellow Christians who can't serve God the way they dream of serving due to health issues. I decided I would do all I could to stay healthy (eating right, staying clean, exercising…) so I can serve God long into my life. The final reason we should practice good hygiene is to be *healthy to serve God*. Write that in the space below.

REASON 3: _____

Look Inside Yourself

On the next page you'll find the meditator girl we used earlier in the book. One who studies and prays generally ends up making wise decisions. This should include the area of taking care of your body. Let's consider her the model of health. On the left side of her, write a list of all the wise choices she makes to be clean and healthy. On the right side of her, write a list of all the things that help you reach your goal of being clean and healthy and growing in those areas.

Meditator's Healthy,
Clean Habits

My Healthy,
Clean Habits

_____   _____

_____   _____

_____   _____

_____   _____

_____   _____

_____   _____

_____   _____

_____   _____

My Healthy, Clean Habit Goals

No one is perfect. Remember Marie's story at the beginning of the chapter? She doesn't want anyone to feel bad about the way they have been taken care of or what they haven't learned yet about hygiene. It's okay if you need to set some goals based on what you learned today. In the space below, write down three goals you can use to start taking better care of yourself.

1. _____

2. _____

3. _____

Reach Up to Talk to GoD

Hi, Jesus!

I'm ready to talk a bit about hygiene and health. I realize that my body is your temple, or house, so I want to take care of it for you. I also want to be able to be around other people and work closely with them, and I know I have to be clean for that. I think / don't think **(circle one)** I'm very healthy. I do have these good habits: _____

_____.

But I could totally stand to work on these things: _____

_____

_____. Can you please teach me how to do this right? Motivate me to stay clean and eat right. Sometimes I can be lazy about that. Help me accept advice from other people about my cleaning habits. I confess that sometimes I get grumpy when people correct me. And most of all, help me to want super clean insides. I want to love you, follow you, serve you, and be like you. That's more about my heart than anything else, so help me make that the most important thing of all!

I really love you,

_____

(sign here)

THE ABCs OF BECOMING A CHRISTIAN

Lots of people say they are Christians, but many of them probably are not. What a sad thing to think that going to church, being good, or calling yourself a Christian would be your ticket to heaven, all the while never having actually chosen to follow Jesus Christ in obedience. Jesus himself said he was the only way to heaven. John 14:6 reads, "Jesus said… 'I am the way, the truth, and the life. No one comes to the Father except through me.'" Becoming a Christian is not difficult, but many people are confused or distracted by things and actions that do not make them Christians any more than walking on all fours makes me a dog!

A **Admit you are a sinner.** A person starts by confessing that she has sinned. She must be sorry for her sin and be willing to stop. Whether you have been fighting with your siblings or cheating on tests (or moms, fighting with your siblings or cheating on your taxes), sin separates us from God. He is so perfect and holy, he cannot be in the presence of uncleansed sin. Romans 3:23 says, "All have sinned and fall short of the glory of God." There's that word again— "glory." We cannot reflect God's image if sin is in us. And this verse says we're all guilty.

If you know you have sinned, pause right now to confess your sin out loud to God.

B **Believe that Jesus is the Son of God and that his death on the cross paid for all your sins.** You may be familiar with John 3:16. That beloved Bible verse reads, "For God so loved the world, that he gave his only Son, that whoever believes in him should not perish but have eternal life." What kind of love is that? That God would sacrifice his only Son so we can live with him. He so wants you to be a Christian because he loves you.

If you believe Jesus is God's Son, pause to say that to him out loud.

C **Confess your faith in Jesus out loud and to others.** Romans 10:9 says, "If you confess with your mouth that Jesus is Lord and believe in your heart that God raised him from the dead, you will be saved." Salvation requires your mouth! You must tell both God and others that Jesus is the Lord of your life.

If you want Jesus to be the Lord of your life, begin by pausing to ask him out loud right now. Then go tell someone! You have become our sister in Jesus today. Welcome to the family!

Your Hair, a Crown

But I want you to understand that the
head of every man is Christ, the head of a wife is her husband,
and the head of Christ is God.

1 CORINTHIANS 11:3

I (Suzy) took piano lessons when I was a tween, but I never wanted to practice. Been there? Without practice, I did not excel. I tried again with the clarinet in high school, and as it turns out, I'm not a bad musician. I sped past a lot of clarinet players during those two years. But then I walked away from music for a long time. Eventually, I married a great musician who soon started recording worship albums. I got a little scared by that. *What if he gets famous? What if he starts traveling all over the country in a band and leaves me home alone?* I didn't want to be left behind!

I decided I'd better pick up an instrument pretty quickly, and I chose drums. My first time behind the kit, I was hooked! I spent hours playing and

playing and playing. Before I knew it, I was playing in churches.
Then I played on a couple of albums, and then I was traveling
around the country with Dannah. At that time, I wasn't known as
an author or a Secret Keeper Girl speaker. I was Dannah's drummer.

Wouldn't you know God had other plans—and he used my hair,
of all things, to make them known! After the very first event where
I played drums, Dannah began to get emails from teenage girls
who wanted to hear more from the "drummer chick with the red
hair." (For the record, it was not natural red, mind you, but full-on,
bright red dye.) The teen girls were not attracted to my hair. It was
only a marker for who I was. They were attracted by the fact that I
was doing what guys usually do—play the drums—but was still an
all-out girl who loved Jesus like crazy. (Remember from meditation
2 that we can be many kinds of girls as long as we remember that
God made us female to reflect his image.)

Dannah came to me one day and said, "I think I need to put
you in front of a microphone and see what happens," and the rest
is Secret Keeper Girl history. My drumming
wasn't about me, nor was my red hair. God
used my hair and my drum skills to lead me
to Secret Keeper Girl and to fulfill his plan to
use me for his kingdom.

le•gal•ism
(noun) • : excessive
conformity to the
law or a religious or
moral code

You see, even our hair is meant for God's
glory! Let's learn more about that while we
take a look at hair care. And this seems a
good time to discuss something controversial
about the way we take care of our beautiful selves—legalism.
Uh-oh—controversy straight ahead.

THE MANE EVENT

Hair care is hard to write about since girls all have different types of hair. Curly. Wavy. Short. Long. Straight. Asian straight. (I [Dannah] have an Asian daughter. Trust me—Asian straight is even straighter than regular straight!) Because of this we can't advise you specifically on how to care for your hair, but we can give you the topics to explore with your mom or big sister. If you get permission, you could even search online for ways to care for your specific hair type. Here are the "mane" things to go over.

girls have all different types of hair!

Washing

Find out how often you should wash your hair based on your hair type. Ask what types of shampoo and conditioner to use and what you need to do before or after you use them. For example, someone with dry, curly hair may have to learn how to detangle it before or after a shampoo.

Drying

Air-drying is always the healthiest choice because it avoids stressing your hair with hot air from a blow dryer. But using a blow dryer is sometimes appropriate because it makes your hair look more finished and clean. Ask someone to teach you how to do that for your hair type. Have fun with it. Learn to straighten it or put more curls into it with a dryer, brush, and products.

Cutting

Based on hair type and finances, how often should you plan to have your hair cut? What are the benefits of cutting it?

Styling! Get some fun ideas of how to style your hair. Here are some snapshots from other Secret Keeper Girls and brief instructions on how to get each look.

① **Alayna • Illusion Mermaid Braid with a twist:** Do a French fishtail braid in the center of the back of your head. Complete about four strands, divide the hair in half and do two fishtail braids. Tuck the ends under and secure at the base of your neck under the braid with bobby pins.

② **Tamara • Waterfall Braid:** Similar to a French braid, but instead of picking up a new piece of hair with each "braid" allow the piece to fall and choose an entirely new piece to incorporate into the braid.

③ **ZaanuYa • Pom-Poms:** Part your hair down the center from forehead to nape of your neck. Gather each part tightly with a ponytail holder directly above each ear (from left to right: Sorochi, Maruchechi, and ZaanuYa).

④ **Carolina • Low Side Ponytail Pinwheel:** A handmade over-the-top embellished elastic headband with hair in a low side ponytail.[1]

meditation 4

Your Hair, a Crown

Do you know what legalism is? It's an overly strict response to laws or rules.

Here's an example. When our church built a new building, our city's laws required us to plant a row of trees to separate our property from a nearby farm. The only thing is, the farm next to our property already had a row of big, tall, evergreen trees. We asked for permission not to plant new ones because they could actually harm the growth of the old ones. But the city said we had to follow the rule and plant the trees. Fast-forward to today—the trees are actually harming each other because they are too close to each other.

That's legalism.

A lot of people try to make legalistic rules about beauty, fashion, and modesty. As teachers who love what the Bible says about these things, we don't like legalism. Today as we discover that even your hair can glorify God, we'll also discover that rules with no reason are not helpful.[2]

DIG IN by Studying 1 Corinthians 11:4-16

Today we're going to read part of a letter the apostle Paul wrote to a church that was struggling with legalism. The church people were fighting about all sorts of things. (That's what happens when you have rules without reason.) One of them was women's hair! (Can you imagine your pastor getting upset about women's hair?) Let's see what we can learn about your body and beauty as we dive into a catfight that still raises the hair on the back of some people's neck!

Getting the facts straight. This letter was written to a church in the Middle East, where covering your head is *still* considered a way of showing respect to those around you and to God. So in that culture, covering your head when you pray is a way to say, "God, you are more important than me." Covering your head in public is not a biblical command—it's a cultural tradition. The church in Corinth believed this was super important, so they wanted Paul to make a hard-and-fast rule that women should always have long hair and always cover their heads when they pray. Let's see what he told them.

4 Any man who speaks with God or about God in a way that shows a lack of respect for the authority of Christ, dishonors Christ. **5** In the same way, a wife who speaks with God in a way that shows a lack of respect for the authority of her husband, dishonors her husband. **6** Worse, she dishonors herself —an ugly sight, like a woman with her head shaved.

This is basically the origin of these customs we have of women wearing head coverings in worship, while men take their hats off. By these symbolic acts, **7-9** men and women, who far too often butt heads with each other, submit their "heads" to the Head: God. **10** Don't, by the way, read too much into the differences here between men and women. **11** Neither man nor woman can go it alone or claim priority. Man was created first, as a beautiful shining reflection of God—that is true. But the head on a woman's body clearly outshines in beauty the head of her "head," her husband.

12 The first woman came from man, true—but ever since then, every man comes from a woman! And since virtually everything comes from God anyway, let's quit going through these "who's first" routines.

13-15 Don't you agree there is something naturally powerful in the symbolism—a woman, her beautiful hair reminiscent of angels, praying in adoration; a man, his head bared in reverence, praying in submission? **16** I hope you're not going to be argumentative about this. All God's churches see it this way; I don't want you standing out as an exception (1 Corinthians 11:4-16 MSG).

Basically, Paul is saying, stop fighting about how to show respect to God and each other and just do it! We all matter. Boys. Girls. Men. Women. Why? **Fill in the blank below.**

We matter because our purpose is to

_____ _____.

We hope you wrote "glorify God." And though we don't think there is a rule for how God wants your hair to be in our culture, we do think that a woman's hair can be used for his glory. It is for God's glory. Everything is for his glory, remember? "Whether you eat or drink, or whatever you do, do all to the glory of God" (1 Corinthians 10:31). "Whatever you do" in this verse even includes styling or cutting your hair!

When Suzy's red hair was calling out from behind the drummer's kit, it was God who was being glorified, not Suzy or her hair. I (Dannah) was there. I know that Suzy's red hair made teen girls want to learn more about that crazy drummer's passion for Jesus!

THINK ABOUT IT

What are some things that are unique about you…hobbies, style, interests, skills? **Write them down. Now write this beneath them:** I'm okay if God uses these things to take me somewhere he wants to lead me!

_____

_____

_____

_____

_____

DON'T PULL YOUR HAIR OUT!

Today's legalistic rules about hair still cause problems. Here are two of them hashed out for your consideration. Talk to your mom about what she thinks. Judge for yourselves!

Is it okay to cut your hair? Some people believe 1 Corinthians 11:15 teaches that we should not cut our hair, but that's not really true. Paul writes, "If a woman has long hair…" The word "if" is implying that it is not a must, but a maybe. A woman might have long hair. She might not. Not everyone has the good fortune of thick, full hair. And some that do wish theirs could be straight and light. Nothing is wrong with cutting your hair into a style that suits your face and figure and makes you feel confident. Our hair is part of our body, so it should be groomed and cared for as part of God's temple. Need a haircut? Snip, snip!

Is it okay to color your hair? The Bible doesn't give us instructions on this, but it does say that gray hair is a crown. Some use the passage to assert that we must never color our hair. You may feel called to let the gray come naturally. Go for it, and let it be your crown. But nowhere does the Bible prohibit hair color. If dying your hair makes you look better and you enjoy the results, grab a box and go for it!

Do what you like with your hair, but be sure you're blessing the Lord in your heart as you do it!

The Bible verse below doesn't make sense. Unscramble it. (Look up the verse if you need help.)

SKG
Puzzle Craze

"righteous hair in a crown of Gray is glory;

it is a gained life" (Proverbs 16:31).

_____

_____

For puzzle answers go to page 118.

What's more important in the verse above? The gray hair or the righteous life? Use your green pen again to circle the answer you choose.

We believe it's the righteous life. Gray hair is a result of a righteous life because those who live well can live longer. (Back in the day when the Bible was written, no one colored their hair. Not red. Not blonde. Not brown. So people's gray hair announced their age...and the wisdom that got them there.)

The point is this: The Bible says our gray hair is a crown displayed to the world that we lived our lives well. How do you live well? By following God's rules. What? Wait a minute—didn't we just say that legalism is getting too strict about rules? Yep, we did. Boy, is this complicated! It's time to look inside ourselves to figure this one out.

Don't get us wrong—God does have rules for us. But most of them have little to do with how we look and much more to do with how we treat others and what's going on inside us. (Sadly, a lot of Christians try to make rules about how we should look. These folks usually mean well, but rules like that often take the focus away from what matters to God the most—our hearts.)

There are three ways to approach things when making decisions about how we present our bodies—hair, nails, fashion, and more. Here they are:

1 LEGALISM—making rules and saying they are God's even though they aren't written in the Bible.

2 A FAIR JUDGMENT—making rules for ourselves, our family, or our church that seem best for us based on what we know about what is written in the Bible, but never forcing others to live by our preferences.

3 GOD'S REAL RULES—God gives us some rules, and we should live by them. These are always written clearly in the Bible, and we can find them in specific Bible passages.

Chose from one of these three options for each scenario below. Put a big smiley face in the correct column every time you come across a scenario that is **a fair judgment** or **God's real rules**. Put a big sad face in the correct column when you sniff out some **legalism**.

	Legalism	A Fair Judgment	God's Real Rules
JEN is not allowed to color her hair red because "Christians don't do that."			
SARAH'S youth group has to wear one-piece swimsuits to the pool party because her youth pastor says that is the "church preference."			
ALISON'S mom tells her that it's not good for a girl to dress like a boy based on Deuteronomy 22:5 but tells her that it can sometimes be hard to tell what is for girls and what is for boys today. She just instructs her to be careful.			

For puzzle answers go to page 118.

If you had a hard time, check the answers in the back of the book on page 118. We tried to make it easy, but now it's going to get harder. We want you to draw a picture in each box below showing the choices YOU have made in these areas.

For example, I (Dannah) once saw a girl with hot pink hair at one of my events. I made a rule in my head that she could not possibly love God because she looked so punky. But she was a great lover of Jesus! In my heart, I was embracing legalism, and I asked God to forgive me.

When my daughter Lexi was in fourth grade, she asked me to color her hair cotton-candy pink. I said yes—that was a "fair judgment" for our family. However, anytime my girls have been tempted to wear something immodest, I turn them to verses in God's Word encouraging women to dress modestly.

What about you?

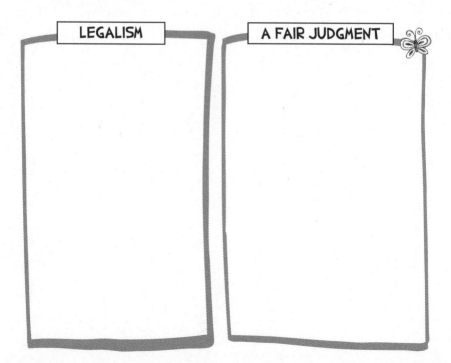

LEGALISM

A FAIR JUDGMENT

GOD'S REAL RULES

Reach Up to Talk to GoD

Hi, Jesus!

Wow! Today I learned about legalism, fair judgments, and your rules. This sounds _____. Help me to understand the difference. I especially ask you to help me to be wise when I see other people and the way they present their hair, faces, or bodies. Help me remember that they may or may not know you and might need me to love them, not correct them. In my family we seem to lean toward **(circle one)** legalism / fair judgments / God's rules. Here is how I think you want me to respond: _____ _____ _____. Please help me to NEVER disobey your rules and to have wisdom to make fair judgments.

Sincerely,

_____

(sign here)

Food, Your Fuel

*And God said, "Behold, I have given you every
plant yielding seed that is on the face of
all the earth, and every tree with seed in
its fruit. You shall have them for food."*
GENESIS 1:29

We have a problem for you to solve in this chapter. Pay close attention because we're going ask you to make a decision for an 11-year-old. We've made her up, but her story might sound like yours or a friend's.

Meet Mandy. She is 11 years old and has always been the heaviest girl in her class. When she had to run the mile for gym class, she felt as if she might puke. She wasn't able to keep running with her class and had to walk to finish it. She started to notice that she didn't have as much energy as her friends when they hung out together. And just this year Mandy started to enter puberty and noticed some big changes in her body. One of the biggest changes was that she grew almost three inches, and that made her start to think!

She asked her mom for some help. Her mom took her to see a doctor to make sure no physical problems were causing the low energy. He confirmed that Mandy's inactivity and her constant diet of cheeseburgers and fries dipped in milkshakes could be slowing her down. With a little bit of nutritional help from her doctor and super coaching from her mom and dad, Mandy lost some weight, gained some energy, and earned a spot on a traveling soccer team. She loves feeling healthy and is able to run long distances without feeling as if she might toss her lunch.

Mandy also loves that the meanest boy in the class doesn't call her names any longer. She still thinks he's mean, but she's not his target. As a bonus, Mandy has found the courage to stand up for others when he picks on them.

This weekend Mandy has been invited to a soccer sleepover. The invitation says there is going to be dancing, dancing, dancing, movies, movies, movies, and food, food, FOOD! She's scared. What if it's all pizza and donuts and candy? What if they have milkshakes and fries—she can hardly say no to those! She has avoided all junk food in favor of fruits and vegetables for almost a year now.

Food and exercise, particularly for girls your age, are hot topics in our world today. We hear a lot about them in the letters we receive at Secret Keeper Girl. Sometimes people ask us, if God looks at the heart and not at outward appearance, why should we care at all if we are overweight? People want to know if we stand behind the fashion magazines that seem to suggest thin = beautiful. The easy answer is NO.

[We don't think thin = beautiful.]

We stand with God in agreeing that beauty is determined way more by what is on the inside than what is on the outside. But we also need to remember that we are to glorify God with our bodies and that our bodies are his temple. If our purpose is to glorify God and he is living in our bodies, then we should take seriously the care and keeping of our bodies. This goes way beyond being thin. It's about being physically fit.

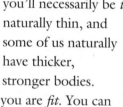

[We do think physically fit = wise.]

It simply isn't wise to risk health by being overweight or by filling yourself with junk food. If the purpose of your body is to glorify God, it has to be strong for the tasks he calls you to do. Besides, God specifically instructed us to glorify him when we eat and drink! (1 Corinthians 10:31). Wisdom says, "Take care of the body God has given you for this amazing ride we call life." Be wise. Pursue fitness. That does *not* mean you'll necessarily be *thin*. Some of us are naturally thin, and some of us naturally have thicker, stronger bodies.

wise

(adjective) • : *having or showing experience, knowledge, or good judgment*

But you'll know when you are *fit*. You can feel it in the strength of your being.

Let's see if our meditation today will help us become wise about being fit. You can become an expert consultant for Mandy— you'll get to advise her later in the chapter. What are we waiting for? Her sleepover is happening soon, so we've got to tell her what to do about it!

meditation 5

Food, Your Fuel

We aren't here to tell you what you should or should not eat. Instead, we're here to help you discover the purpose of food and how to achieve that purpose. From there, we'll trust you to use your own judgment—just as the apostle Paul trusted the Corinthian church to judge for themselves whether women's hair should be long or short. That's kind of how food works.

One big reason for this is that everyone's body is different. Therefore, some things that seem perfectly healthy to one person can make another person not feel well. Wheat, for example, makes me (Dannah) feel tired, not strong. I'm not allergic to it. I've been tested. But when I create MyPlate, it includes a lot more veggies and a whole lot fewer grains. (I have to get my grains from oatmeal, beans, Ezekiel bread, and stuff like that.) But I have also decided that a wood-fired cheese pizza from my favorite local restaurant is okay now and then. I am avoiding legalism and using judgment. (See how we're using your vocab words from last lesson? NICE!) Okay, with that settled, let's dig in.

DIG IN by Studying Genesis 9:1-5

Today we're diving in to the Bible at the very end of the story of Noah and the ark. I (Dannah) would have been a fantastic Mrs. Noah. I love my animals. I have 20 to be exact. Two horses, two fainting goats, two cats, seven llamas, one miniature donkey, three peacocks, and two chickens. Oh, and let's not forget Moose, my labradoodle, who is snoring under my feet as I type these words to you. Living on a farm fulfills my dream of becoming a veterinarian. I get to play with the animals and care for them.

Sometimes I think about what life would have been like before Noah's flood. You see, the animals were apparently rather tame before the flood, which may explain why Noah and wife had no problem getting them into the ark! But after the flood, everything changed.

Use a brown marker to circle all the different types of critters that are mentioned in the passage below. (*Hint: There are four.*)

1 God blessed Noah and his sons and said

to them, "Be fruitful and multiply and fill the earth.

2 The fear of you and the dread of you shall be upon

every beast of the earth and upon every bird of the heavens,

upon everything that creeps on the ground and all the

fish of the sea. Into your hand they are delivered.

3 Every moving thing that lives shall be food for you.

And as I gave you the green plants, I give you everything.

4 But you shall not eat flesh with its life, that is, its blood.

5 And for your lifeblood I will require a reckoning:

from every beast I will require it and from man.

From his fellow man I will require a reckoning

for the life of man (Genesis 9:1-5).

Use a black or gray marker to draw a square around the two words that describe how these critters are going to feel about humans after the flood.

I guess if I were a big old juicy salmon or a nice fat beef cow, I'd have "fear" and "dread" of you if you were going to eat me too! Isn't it interesting that humans didn't always eat meat? Did you know that? For thousands of years, humans had been instructed by God to limit themselves to green plants.

Use a green marker to draw a heart around the thing that humans ate before the flood.

humans didn't always eat meat!

Before the flood, humans were primarily vegetarians. Our bodies today are classified as omnivores (able to digest both meat and vegetables), but God's original instructions to humans were to eat veggies. We must need them! Carnivores— those created to eat meat, such as wolves—have very short intestinal tracts, so meat can go through them quickly without getting stuck in there and rotting. Vegetarians—those created to eat vegetation, such as cows—have longer intestinal tracts, so food goes through them slowly. What do you think humans have? **Write it below.**

_____

_____

That's right! God created us with longer intestinal tracts. In the very beginning, God instructed Adam and Eve what they should eat based on how he constructed our bodies: "And God said, 'Behold, I have given you every plant yielding seed that is on the face of all the earth, and every tree with seed in its fruit. You shall have them for food'" (Genesis 1:29).

Why did God change his directions after the flood? Some Bible scholars think that there was no vegetation to eat, so God made this allowance. The fact is, avoiding meat isn't right or wrong. It's just wise. God makes lots of allowances for us when it comes to food, but we were designed to eat the stuff he grows—vegetables, fruits, and whole grains. Those should make up the bulk of our diet.

Over time, we have adapted to needing and getting our protein from animal products, such as eggs, meats, and dairy products. So these should now also be an important part of our diet.

What shouldn't be in our diet in excess? Hmm…maybe we should talk about that too.

Look Inside Yourself

We each like certain foods—a lot. I (Suzy) never pass up a Sonic, and if there were only one bad breakfast food on earth, I would want it to be powdered donuts. I (Dannah) think McDonald's has mastered the French fry, and if there were one last dessert left on earth, it should be a hot fudge sundae! We like that God makes allowances for what we eat. (Remember the word "legalism" from the last chapter? When it comes to food, we are not legalists!)

Use one of the boxes below to draw the logo of your favorite fast-food restaurant. (Rest assured you, we're not getting paid to advertise anyone. We just want to make a point.) And use one of the boxes below to draw your favorite junk food.

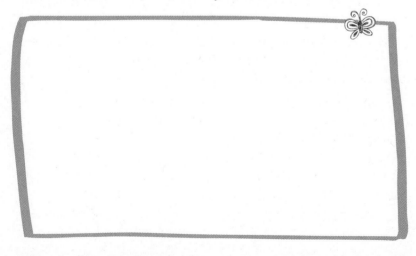

Now write "It's okay!" inside each box. Unless you have a medical condition that forbids you to eat that stuff, it's an acceptable allowance. But remember, it's wise to be fit.

Here are a few things that are not wise for the human body. Circle any that you may be guilty of.

- getting a sunburn
- going on a diet that causes rapid weight loss
- withholding food entirely
- overexercising
- bingeing on candy
- bingeing on soda

- eating only junk food
- eating no fruits, vegetables, or whole grains
- using drugs
- getting drunk
- smoking

A wise girl doesn't do any of these things to her body and tries to break any bad habits that have crept in. She also takes care not to be too extreme about anything. Not too much junk food. And not being overly strict (legalistic) about health food. One of our favorite Bible verses says, "Whoever fears God will avoid all extremes" (Ecclesiastes 7:18 NIV). It's time to put your expert-consultant hat on and help Mandy. Based on that, what would you tell Mandy to do this weekend?

A Just relax. Eat what you want and what you like, but only when you are feeling hungry.

B Either pack a bunch of veggies in your bag or plan on starving. You don't want to go back to that lifestyle!

C Eat up, girl! You never know when you'll have the perfect excuse to eat all the junk food you want again. Besides, one night never hurt anyone.

What did you pick based on everything you've learned in this lesson? For the record, we would advise Mandy to go with choice A. The problem with choice B and the problem with choice C is exactly the same. Whether Mandy is afraid to eat anything but a carrot (choice B) or goes crazy with junk food (choice C), she is letting food *control* her.

We don't want to be controlled by anything but God's Holy Spirit. On the other hand, we also want to be sure we are not careless or lazy. When Mandy was struggling with her weight, she could have said, "God loves me just the way I am, and that is good enough for me." Did God love her just the way she was? You bet! Did he have better plans for her? You know he did!

Mandy should be pretty excited about the fact that she worked hard and was rewarded by feeling better and winning a spot on a good soccer team.

FOOD IS FUEL

You gain wisdom about your body in two ways. First, as your care for your body, you experience consequences—both good and bad. Second, wisdom also comes from knowledge, which we hope to give you in the next two chapters. From these things you are able to use good judgment. (Remember that word from our last chapter?) Let's get wise.

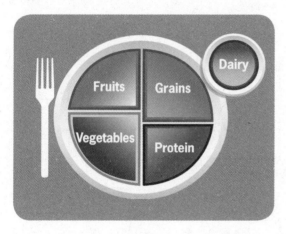

Just as a car requires gasoline to run, our bodies require fuel to run. But in our Western culture, we think of food as entertainment, not fuel. Cinnamon rolls. Butterfinger Blizzards. French fries. Pizza. These are staples for many people, but they won't give us energy. If you want energy, you need carrots, whole wheat toast, bananas, blueberries, and spinach. The US government has designed this simple MyPlate graphic so you can see what each meal should look like.

There is a copy of this with a Bible verse and eating plan on the last page of this chapter so you can cut it out and put it somewhere to monitor how well you are using food as fuel.

SKG
Puzzle Craze

Your diet doesn't have to be restricted to these things. (Remember, God makes allowances.) But the things in this puzzle should be eaten more than anything else.

ACROSS

6. World's biggest fruits
7. A princess once slept on one of these

DOWN

1. They help with vision
2. Red veggies that are really fruits
3. Chinese staple that's white
4. A Veggie Tale Madame
5. These are good baked and loaded

For puzzle answers go to page 118.

Now, let's make a few of those foods more fun by matching them up to some partners that could create some really yummy after-school or bedtime snacks. Using three of the things you've just found in the crossword puzzle, fill in the blanks below:

peanut butter and _____

_____ and ranch dip

_____ and whipped cream

Since this is all about judgment, there's really no right or wrong answers for what you wrote above. **If you like peanut butter and peas, who are we to judge?**

THINK ABOUT IT

What foods make me feel great? Which ones often make me feel a little sick to my tummy? Make a short list below. What do you think? Do you always have to avoid the "sick to my tummy" list?

_____

_____

_____

_____

_____

_____

Hi, Jesus!

Reach Up to Talk to GOD

I knew / didn't know **(circle one)** that you originally told humans to eat vegetables, fruits, and grains. It's good to know that you make allowances, like when you let Noah eat meat. Here are a few things I'd like to eat as allowances: _____, _____, _____, and _____. And here are a few things you created me to eat that I like a lot: _____, _____, _____, and _____. Thanks for making these for me. Help me to never be too extreme in how I eat—I want to be fit for your glory. Give me self-control when I need it and wisdom to approach what I eat with good judgment.

Sincerely,

_____

(sign here)

Fuel Yourself for His Glory

So whether you eat or drink or whatsoever you do, **do it all for the glory of God.** 1 CORINTHIANS 10:31

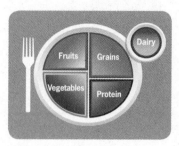

Keep track of how well you fuel yourself for one week. Simply color a Secret Keeper Girl daisy each time you eat something in that specific food group. At the end of the week, add up the daisies to see how well you have done.

TOTALS

GRAINS ✿ ✿ ✿ ✿ ✿ ✿ ✿ ✿ ✿ ✿
✿ ✿ ✿ ✿ ✿ ✿ ✿ ✿ ✿ ✿ ____

VEGETABLES ✿ ✿ ✿ ✿ ✿ ✿ ✿
✿ ✿ ✿ ✿ ✿ ✿ ✿ ✿ ✿ ____

PROTEINS ✿ ✿ ✿ ✿ ✿ ✿ ✿ ✿ ✿
✿ ✿ ✿ ✿ ✿ ✿ ✿ ✿ ✿ ____

FRUITS ✿ ✿ ✿ ✿ ✿ ✿ ✿ ✿ ✿ ✿
✿ ✿ ✿ ✿ ✿ ✿ ✿ ✿ ✿ ✿ ____

DAIRY ✿ ✿ ✿ ✿ ✿ ✿ ✿ ✿ ✿ ✿
✿ ✿ ✿ ✿ ✿ ✿ ✿ ✿ ✿ ✿ ____

Secret Keeper Girl
secretkeepergirl.com

6

Exercise, Your Strength

I discipline my body and keep it under control.
1 CORINTHIANS 9:27

I (Dannah) have to admit that when I read what Suzy wrote about Mandy in the last chapter, I felt conviction. You know, that feeling you get when you know God is telling you something isn't good for you and you shouldn't do it. Why did I feel that? Because if I had been invited to that sleepover party, there is no question in my mind that I would have used it as an excuse to eat anything I wanted and then some! I kid you not! I really struggle with knowing when to say no to yummy food. Once when I was about ten, I ate so many noodles that my parents had to help me stand up after I was finished!

I face a similar battle when it comes to working out. I will look for any excuse NOT to be active. I like to read, sit quietly, watch TV, and play with my animals. But I don't like to run, play ball, or get competitive the way that Suzy does. Let me share a secret that has helped me a lot with how I look at food and exercise. Galatians 5:17 says, "The desires of the flesh are against the Spirit, and the desires of the Spirit are against the flesh, for these are opposed to each other, to keep you from doing the things you want to do." Every single day, a battle is raging between your flesh and the Spirit of the living God.

Two teachers I have enjoyed, Jenny and Taylor Gallman, once put it this way: Your spirit (which houses God's Spirit) and your flesh are like two sumo wrestlers. The one you feed the most will always be stronger and will always win. Feeding your spirit and making your flesh serve God and submit to him in little things assures you that you'll win in the big things.

We feed our flesh (our body) by sleeping in late, overeating, watching television shows that aren't good for us, procrastinating when we have homework to do, and being too lazy to brush our teeth.

self-con•trol

(noun) • : control over your feelings or actions; controlling yourself

We feed our spirit when we get up early to read our Bibles, eat veggies when we want donuts, turn the television off when it gets nasty, do our homework before we hang out, and take good care of our teeth.

These are just some simple examples, but you get the idea. Feeding our flesh fuels selfishness. Feeding our spirit fuels self-control.

Our flesh does not naturally desire to do things that glorify God, but it will easily work to dishonor him. That's why we struggle so much with sin and temptation. Left to our own devises, we sleep in instead of getting up to read our Bible. We watch television shows that train our mind to laugh at sin rather than to honor God by thinking of things that are pure. We indulge in too much junk food rather than having the conviction of self-control…and the list goes on and on. Instead of glorifying God with our bodies, we do a great deal to deny him. What I want you to hear is this:

[Your spirit has a job to do—to glorify God!— so your body better get its attitude straight!]

Suzy loves working out and has a great attitude about it. Recently, she even got me up two mornings a week to work out with her at six thirty. Now that's amazing—and I feel so good!

meditation 6

Exercise, Your Strength

I t is true that I (Suzy) am always ready for some competition with a ball. And recently, I've been running competitively in 5K races and training for a triathlon. This is every bit as fun for me as reading a book. I love it, but not everyone does, and that's okay.

I want to be clear that our weight and our fitness have absolutely nothing to do with our salvation. Heaven will be full of people who were too thin, just right, physically fit, and flat-out flabby. But our weight and fitness may have some impact on our ability to serve God (to glorify him) while we are here on earth. I don't know about you, but I want to serve God as energetically as I can and for as long as I can. I want God to say, "Well done, good and faithful servant!" about every aspect of my life here on earth, including how I took care of my body.

Let's dig in and see if we can get some wisdom from the Bible on what God thinks of fitness.

DIG IN by Studying 1 Corinthians 9:24-27

One of my favorite guys in the Bible is the apostle Paul. Not only did God use him to say some of the most challenging things ever written, but Paul and I have a hobby in common—sports. Paul made it as clear as daylight in the letters he wrote that he was a big sports fan. His letters mention wrestling, boxing, running, throwing…all the big sports of his day. Paul compared our training as ones who love Jesus to the training of an athlete. Using a marker the color of your favorite sports team, circle every instance in the Bible verses below that refers to any sport.

24 Do you not know that in a race all the runners run,

but only one receives the prize? So run that you may obtain it.

25 Every athlete exercises self-control in all things.

They do it to receive a perishable wreath, but we an

imperishable. **26** So I do not run aimlessly; I do not box as

one beating the air. **27** But I discipline my body and

keep it under control, lest after preaching to others I myself

should be disqualified (1 Corinthians 9:24-27).

Paul is not saying that running is spiritual, and he's not saying that boxing is the secret to a happy Christian life. These are word pictures that help us understand how we should be living our spiritual lives—like athletes who work hard because there is a prize to be won. We should be training hard to win the prize of pleasing God.

Look at verse 25 and circle the word that every athlete exercises. (Hint: It's not their legs, abs, or lungs, but something you can't see.) Use the word you find to fill in the blank.

[The main reason we should exercise our bodies is to practice]

_____ _____.

The answer to that is simple:
self-control.

Overeating and lack of exercise are both problems with self-control. Self-control is a fruit of the Holy Spirit (it should be present in every Christian). Your life and mine should be full of self-control.

The way Dannah and I look at exercise is very different from the way a lot of other people do. We don't think it is primarily about getting physically fit (although we mentioned in the last chapter that being physically fit is wise). Exercise is primarily about developing self-control so that your spirit—not your body—is in control of your decisions.

SKG
Puzzle Craze

Get your artist on, girl. You're going to grab all of your markers and draw two very different pictures in the boxes below. One is based on what a life without self-control looks like and one is based on what a life with self-control looks like. Using the Bible verses in each box, draw a picture.

NO SELF-CONTROL Proverbs 5:23 NLT

SELF-CONTROL 1 Corinthians 9:25

A life of no self-control is ugly and full of stress and destruction. But a life of self-control provides for peace and reward. Which one are you choosing?

Look Inside Yourself

Meet Greedy Greta, Gluttonous Gabby, and Lazy Luna. These are the characters that take over our body when we don't exercise self-control. Let's figure out if any of them are taking up space inside of you.

GREEDY GRETA: "I'm Greta, and I can't get enough stuff—clothes, money, friends, attention, food...I love it all. Sometimes people who are greedy are called 'fat cats,' but I don't like that nickname. I'm not fat. What does fat have to do with it? I just like to have as much of everything as I can have. I figure that in the end, life is measured by how much we end up owning."

Is Greedy Greta inside of you? If so, here's a Bible verse to consider. Read it and write a letter to Greedy Greta, telling her to get out!

> Then he [Jesus] said to them, "Watch out! Be on your guard against all kinds of greed; life does not consist in an abundance of possessions" (Luke 12:15 NIV).

Write Greta a quick little note. Use Luke 12:15, and be as kind but as firm as possible. Greta needs a new outlook! Where does she have mistaken ideas? Where might her "stinking thinking" lead her in the future?

 _____

_____

_____

_____

GLUTTONOUS GABBY: "Hey there! I see what you said to Greta, but I'm not nearly as bad as she is. I'm Gabby, and generally speaking, I just like food. Admit it—food is good. I'm always afraid if I don't eat it now I won't be able to get it later, so I make sure I get all I want. The beautiful thing is, I'm not a fat cat either! I can eat and eat and eat…all I want. It's what I live for."

Do you recognize Gabby? If so, read the Bible verse below and write a letter telling her to vacate your heart and mind and body!

> For, as I have often told you before and now tell you again even with tears, many live as enemies of the cross of Christ. Their destiny is destruction, their god is their stomach, and their glory is in their shame. Their mind is set on earthly things (Philippians 3:18-19 NIV).

Write Gabby, using Philippians 3:19. Maybe it would be good for Gabby to see that gluttony isn't about size, but about attitudes of the heart. Is food for nourishing healthy bodies? Or is food supposed to taste good and make us do a happy dance? Maybe you can help Gabby find a couple of things more important in life than yummy food.

 _____

_____

_____

_____

_____

_____

is food a happy dance?

NEWTON'S FIRST LAW OF MOTION

states that an object in motion tends to remain in motion, and an object at rest tends to remain at rest. What does that say about you?

LAZY LUNA: "Hey there! I'm Luna—Lazy Luna, and I'm proud of it too. Why not take it easy? I have all I need. I live in a nice house with a housekeeper (my mom). She cooks all my meals and makes my bed. I pretty much watch TV whenever I'm not forced to be in school. I don't do much homework because I'm smart enough to get A's on my tests. Life is boring, but it's easy. Gotta go—my fave reality TV show is just starting."

Does this sound all too familiar? It's time to apply the Bible verses below to your life and write a letter to Luna.

A little sleep, a little slumber,
a little folding of the hands to rest—
and poverty will come on you like a thief
and scarcity like an armed man (Proverbs 6:10-11).

Diligent hands will rule,
but laziness ends in forced labor (Proverbs 12:24).

That should give you plenty of background information to write your letter to Luna now. Maybe you can help Luna see what her future looks like if she refuses to get off of that couch!

_____

_____

_____

_____

Reach Up to Talk to GoD

Jesus,

This was a tough one to take!

Just between you and me, I can be honest though. I know you know me inside and out, so why not? I do / do not **(circle one)** struggle with weight. I do / do not **(circle one)** make an effort to exercise. I do / do not **(circle one)** pay attention to what I eat. I am / am not **(circle one)** exercising self-control. I know these things matter. I know the world is watching, and I know that if you live in me and I have a relationship with you, I'll look more and more like you all the time—and that includes self-control. I don't want to love my appetites and my stomach (or my couch and my TV shows) more than I love you. I also don't want to make big promises I can't keep, so help me start small. For the next 21 days, I want to do these two things so I can grow in self-control over food and exercise. I'm going to _____ and _____. And I'm going to tell my mom / my dad / another adult **(circle one)** about it so they can keep asking me how it's going! I've got this…with you, that is.

All my love,

_____

(sign here)

Spirit Versus Body Challenge

Exercise works best in pairs. Ask your mom to exercise with you for five days. Try reading the Bible before you do so you can remember it's really about your spirit and self-control, not your body. (If your mom has a copy of *8 Great Dates for Moms and Daughters*, she has a copy of this challenge and some devotions you can do together.)

Sign this Spirit Versus Body Challenge with your mom. Post it on your fridge or the bathroom mirror so you can both see it every day when you are getting ready for the day.

 I discipline my body and keep it under control
(1 Corinthians 9:27).

Every day for the next five days, we, _____ and

_____, will do some quiet prayer and Bible reading

and then exercise for _____ minutes. If one of us misses a day,

that person will _____ for the other.

Here are some things you can do for each other if you miss more than two days:

- 💜 clean the other person's closet
- 💜 give them a foot rub and pedicure
- 💜 walk the dog when it's their turn
- 💜 do the dishes while the other one relaxes

Signed: _____ *Date:* _____

Signed: _____ *Date:* _____

Spirit Versus Body Challenge

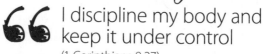 I discipline my body and keep it under control
(1 Corinthians 9:27)

Keep track of the discipline of your body for the next 21 days. Under each day of the week, enter the miles you walk or run. Any exercise you do for 15 minutes counts as one mile. If it's a slow activity, such as golf, it counts as walking. If it is a fast activity, such as basketball, it counts as running.

	WEEK 1	WEEK 2	WEEK 3
MONDAY			
TUESDAY			
WEDNESDAY			
THURSDAY			
FRIDAY			
SATURDAY			
SUNDAY			

Your Body, a Source of Life

When a woman is giving birth, she is has sorrow because her hour has come, but when she has delivered the baby, she no longer remembers the anguish, for joy that a human being has been born into the world.
JOHN 16:21

Have you ever seen a photograph of a baby that's still inside of its mother's belly? Amazing! It's really one of the most amazing photos you can imagine—but you don't have to imagine today. Ask your mom to help you search "photos of fetus" online, and you'll discover that cameras have actually documented the miracle of life inside a mother's womb. As we pointed out in chapter 1, all the changes in your body are happening for a reason—God is preparing your body to make babies. Period.

Speaking of periods, let's dedicate this entire chapter to that change because it's the one girls usually have the most questions about. We're here to answer them. (And if we miss one, you can always hack your mom's Facebook page—with her permission—and write to us.)

meditation 7

Your Body, a Source of Life

Sometimes it's helpful just to hear the basics, so let's start by looking inside. Our other lessons did this metaphorically, looking at our hearts and emotions, but this one is going to literally look inside—at your reproductive system!

Inside of you is a complex, life-giving network called the women's reproductive system. It looks like this:

Female Reproductive System

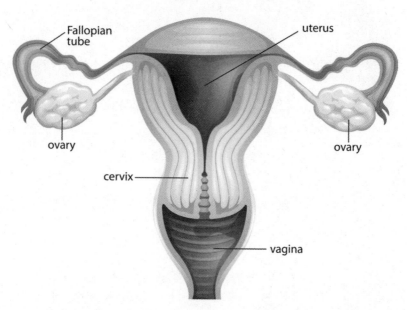

Fallopian tube

uterus

ovary

ovary

cervix

vagina

Until now, it's been growing and being healthy and waiting for you to get big enough to put it to work. That time is now. Beginning very soon, your menstrual cycle is going to begin. This is a monthly cycle in which your body prepares to have a baby, just in case it's time. The cycle looks a little like this:

1 Every month, one egg develops and leaves one of the ovaries. (The ovaries take turns and only have to work every other month.) This is called ovulation. Inside one of the ovaries, draw a tiny happy-faced egg with a pink marker.

2 The egg travels toward the uterus by way of the fallopian tubes. Draw arrows directing the egg out of the ovary and all the way to the uterus.

3 The uterus gets ready to receive the egg by making a thick lining to protect it. Use your red marker and draw a thick line all around the inside of the uterus.

4 A period happens when an egg is released from the ovaries and arrives at the uterus but isn't fertilized to become a baby. Instead of implanting itself in the cozy, thick lining of the uterus, the egg dissolves. This signals the uterus to shed its lining as blood through the vagina. Using your red marker, draw a flow of blood from the uterus through the cervix and out of the opening of the vagina.

Congratulations! You just simulated your first period.

A period will last from two to seven days because only a little bit of blood comes out at a time, especially on your first few. It will happen once every 21 to 45 days, with the average being every 28 days. But everyone has her own "regular" cycle. Talk to your mom about yours until you figure out what is normal for you.

FIVE SIGNS THAT YOUR PERIOD IS COMING

No one can tell you for sure when your period is coming, and every girl's body develops at its own pace. The timing is based on various factors, including your skin and eye color, your nutrition, and how active you might be. Some girls experience no warning signs, but these things signal that most girls' first period will arrive soon.

Breast buds. The first sign that you're going to be fully "woman" soon is thickening in your nipples. It's time to go bra shopping! In most cases this happens about one year before you get your first period—more or less.

Pubic hair. When you go to the bathroom, you'll notice hair growing down there. Not a thing you need to do about this particular change.

Vaginal discharge. Sometimes the body starts cleansing itself before you get your first period. (This happens every month once your cycle begins.) You may notice a small amount of white or clear discharge in your panties. That's okay. Tell your mom if it is yellow or dark or if it smells bad, because that's not okay.

Body weight. Most girls will not start their period until they weigh at least 100 pounds. That's why athletes and dancers sometimes start their period when they are a tad older.

Mood changes. Some girls notice that about a year before they get their first period, they start to feel tired or even a little grumpy about once a month. This can be your body working harder and doing practice drills.

DIG IN by Studying Genesis 3:16; Psalm 127:3-5; John 16:21

Sometimes grown women joke about their period, calling it "the curse." There's a biblical basis for that joke. Use your red marker again to circle the word "pain" below.

I will sharpen the pain of your pregnancy, and in pain you will give birth. And you will desire to control your husband, but he will rule over you (Genesis 3:16 NLT).

Having a baby hurts, and pregnancy is often uncomfortable, but most women are excited when they find out they're going to have a baby.

You might have some cramps every single month you have a period. This is not God's original plan. It's part of the curse we read about in the book of Genesis.

It helps to think about the order in which things happened in the Garden of Eden. God created the earth, and he created man. At first, Adam didn't have to work very hard to get the land to grow things. The land was healthy and produced plenty of green food for Adam and Eve. God had created animals too, but none of them was the perfect partner for man. So God created us women! Of course, there was only one woman at first—Eve.

men•stru•a•tion

(noun) • *: the periodic discharge of blood and tissue from the uterus occurring monthly; your period*

Then Adam and Eve sinned. They ate a piece of forbidden fruit. (The problem was not that they ate the fruit but that they disobeyed God.) God explained that their sin disrupted his plans and laws for relationship and life. (Kind of like jumping off a building would disrupt the law of gravity and create bad consequences when you hit the ground.) God explained that Adam would now have to work hard and sweat a lot to make the ground grow food. He told Eve that her body would find being pregnant and giving birth very painful. Both were curses to be sure…the loss of God's intended plan and blessing.

God had a plan to fix the mess. It included the birth of a little boy, his Son, and God was going use women to accomplish that. Every great person who has ever lived, including our Savior (and including you!), has been born out of a woman. Our bodies are still a part of God's wonderful plan!

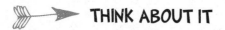 THINK ABOUT IT

To be blessed is to live under God's supernatural power as it works *for* us. To be cursed is to be out from under that protection, where the forces of evil and sin can work *against* us.

Here's the thing. Jesus came for us. He was born, and he died in the place of our sins so we can be under God's blessing once again. Some things haven't changed—we still have to work hard to have food, we still get monthly cramps, and it still hurts to have a baby—but God's plan is to redeem us. Look at this verse and circle all the words that describe what children are to their parents. (Hint: They begin with "h", "f", "a" and one with a "b.")

> **3** Behold, children are a heritage from the LORD,
>
> the fruit of the womb a reward. **4** Like arrows in the hand of
>
> a warrior are the children of one's youth. **5** Blessed is the man
>
> who fills his quiver with them! (Psalm 127:3-5).

We adult women may joke around and call our monthly period "the curse," but what do we call you kiddos? Hint: Unscramble this word. G-L-S-B-E-S-N-I. Now finish this sentence:

I'm a ___ __ __ __ __ __ __ __ to my parents!

God's good plan reverses the curse beautifully. What was cursed is now a blessing. And here's some really good practical news in case the idea of childbirth makes you sweat more than Adam the day God showed him his first field to plow! Use a red marker (representing Christ's blood) to cross out every word in the first part of this Bible verse. Then use a bright yellow (happy) marker to circle the entire second part.

When a woman is giving birth,

she has sorrow because her hour has come...

...but when she has delivered the baby, she no longer

remembers the anguish, for joy that a human being

has been born into the world (John 16:21).

Take it from me (Dannah) that delivering a baby is some of the most fun I've ever had in life. Was it hard work? Yes, but what miraculous hard work! The most God-like thing I've ever done or experienced is childbirth. And as for forgetting the pain? It's almost immediate. The joy overpowers the pain.

Think through all of this as you approach your first period. It could change your attitude about it from *blah* to *yahoo*! Cramps and pads are going to be inconvenient, but keeping the big picture in mind makes it all worthwhile. **Speaking of pads, let's get some practice with our puzzle craze today.**

SKG
Puzzle Craze

We live near Hershey, Pennsylvania—as in Hershey's chocolate kisses. Maybe every city should have a chocolate factory because chocolate is a good thing for a girl who is having her period. You'll also need to have a few other good things on hand when you start your period. You might want to keep one set of these at home and one set at school just in case. Find the following words and circle them in red.

BODY SPRAY   HEATING PAD   MIDOL   TAMPONS
CHOCOLATE   MAXI PADS   MINI PADS

```
V  Q  C  U  I  G  N  C  D  E  V  O  C  B  P
G  B  O  D  Y  S  P  R  A  Y  H  A  L  T  R
L  O  D  I  M  F  T  Z  P  E  S  T  U  K  Z
Z  D  R  S  Q  A  R  R  G  B  Z  O  U  B  G
W  M  R  B  M  M  Z  U  N  H  Z  R  X  W  E
Y  N  A  P  R  D  N  L  I  X  K  Z  D  T  P
E  L  O  X  E  Q  J  D  T  E  L  H  A  Q  G
A  N  L  M  I  R  V  H  A  T  U  L  N  L  B
S  W  S  I  X  P  T  Y  E  F  O  E  T  P  Q
G  T  Z  N  G  A  A  R  H  C  V  F  B  H  C
P  S  E  I  E  H  G  D  O  C  H  Q  K  F  E
N  I  Y  P  W  U  H  H  S  W  B  U  D  Y  C
D  W  X  A  C  V  C  E  B  L  P  S  E  D  M
E  S  F  D  Q  W  F  E  M  M  D  B  W  F  S
Q  V  U  S  B  O  G  E  X  E  E  I  A  K  W
```

For puzzle answers go to page 118.

There are more methods than those in the word search for caring for your period. Some women really like tampons, and others have strong reasons for not using them. We suggest you sit down with your mom, ask what she recommends, and trust her advice.

BRA SHOPPING 101

Getting your first bra can be a ton of fun. Here are three things you need to remember when you go.

1 Get measured. A bra is more comfortable if it is the correct size. You can make sure you buy the right one by measuring yourself and doing a little easy math. Use a tape measure on your rib cage just below the bust to get your band width. This will be something like 28 or 30 inches. The measurement is the size. No need to convert or do math. This may be the only measurement you need. If your breasts have really developed, you'll need to also measure yourself for a cup size. (A cup is what they call the round part that holds in each breast.) For cup size, measure yourself all around at the fullest part of the breast and then subtract the band measurement. A difference of

let's go bra shopping!

half an inch or less is AA. One half to one inch is A, and so on. So if your rib cage measurement is 28 and your breast measurement is 29, you need a size A.

2 Try them on! Everyone does it. We try on bras in the dressing rooms. This saves a lot of frustration and time when you get home and find that the cute one you loved doesn't fit or isn't comfortable. (Even with measurements, you can find differences in the size based on the style.)

3 **Remember the purpose of a bra.** Today's fashion world says that a bra is to make your breasts more noticeable. There are even "meant to be seen" bras that have fancier straps or lace edging. Frankly, it's called *under*wear for a reason. It's mean to be *under* your clothes. A bra should make your breasts a little less noticeable and contained, not more noticeable.

If we could, we'd add this extra piece of advice when bra shopping: Get some ice cream when you're done!

Reach Up to Talk to GOD

Dear God,

I have a lot of questions about my body, but today I feel like I got some answers. What I've heard about my period before made me feel _____, but after studying I feel

_____. I want to go on record to say that it is amazing that you've equipped my body to create new life. Help me to have a good attitude about getting my period. I know that I can always come to you to pray about anything from cramps to bra shopping. Thank you for going through everything with me. I am going to choose to celebrate my body today.

Yippee!

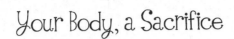

Your Body, a Sacrifice

*I appeal to you therefore, brothers, by the mercies of God,
to present your bodies as a living sacrifice, holy and acceptable
to God, which is your spiritual worship. Do not be conformed
to this world, but be transformed by the renewal of your mind,
that by testing you may discern what is the will of God,
what is good and acceptable and perfect.*

ROMANS 12:1-2

Let's say you loaned me (Suzy) your most valuable possession. It could be something like your iTouch, but maybe it's a precious pet. Whatever it is, I would know one thing for sure—it doesn't belong to me. It belongs to you, and you paid for it. If I were watching your dog for you, I would have to feed it what you told me to feed it and keep it on the exercise schedule you determined. I wouldn't dare have it shaved or tattooed.

I wouldn't take it on a 15-mile run in the blazing sun or make it sleep outside in the bitter cold. I would love it and care for it because it would be yours, and when you returned for your precious pup, you would want to find it just the way you left it—healthy, well cared for, and loved the way you would love it.

Guess what? God has entrusted *you* with one of *his* most valuable possessions—your body! How well are you caring for it?

meditation 8

Your Body, a Living Sacrifice

 y friends make fun of me all the time. And it's okay. I can take it. The thing is, I'm just doing what my mom taught me to do.

I travel a lot, often with friends. Hotel rooms are supposed to be great for jumping on the bed, eating in bed, leaving stuff all over the place, and leaving the bed unmade, right? Well, my mom taught me not to do any of those things...even in a hotel room! I wipe down the counters after using the bathroom. If I'm staying more than one day...well, I wouldn't say I "make" the bed, but I straighten it. I don't wear my shoes on the carpet. And I don't even leave clothes laying around! Why in the world did my mom teach me such crazy habits?

sac•ri•fice

(noun) • : the act of giving up something that you want to keep especially in order to help someone; an offering pleasing to God

Well, she would often explain when I was young that the hotel didn't belong to us, but it did belong to someone who had invested a lot of money in it. And while hotels don't expect counters to be wiped down or beds to be made, someone had to do those things. Would I want to come in to work and have to clean up after gross, inconsiderate people?

Mom's words stuck. I want people to take care of my things, so I should take care of other people's things as well. And get this— since most of my hotel rooms are booked under the name of Secret Keeper Girl, do you think my decisions make SKG look good or bad? It's good for our reputation to take care of things, isn't it?

DIG IN by studying Romans 12:1-2; 1 Corinthians 6:19-20

If you've learned anything about your body during our time together, we hope you've learned to use your body to glorify God. We've come full circle, and it's time to look once again at the Bible verse we began with. Grab your green marker (because green is the color of American money) and underline the words "high price."

Don't you realize that your body is the temple of the Holy Spirit, who lives in you and was given to you by God? You do not belong to yourself, for God bought you with a high price. So you must honor God with your body (1 Corinthians 6:19-20 NLT).

Now use your green marker to circle the name of the one who paid the high price.

Why honor God with our bodies? Because they do not belong to us. They belong to him. He bought you with a high price. Remember, you were a slave to sin. You were separated from God, and the wages for your sin was death. But when Jesus gave his blood on the cross as payment for your sins, he settled the debt you owed to God. He bought you back, and now you belong to him.

Are you taking good care of God's possession? Are you giving your body back to him in service and worship?

Read the verse below and circle the word "bodies" with the green marker. Then circle the two words that describe how we are to present them to God.

1 I appeal to you therefore, brothers, by the mercies of God,

to present your bodies as a living sacrifice, holy and acceptable

to God, which is your spiritual worship. **2** Do not be conformed to

this world, **3** but be transformed by the renewal of your mind,

that by testing you may discern what is the will of God,

what is good and acceptable and perfect (Romans 12:1).

it means we give up our own will

We are supposed to give our bodies back to God as a "living sacrifice." A sacrifice is something that is important to you and that you give up to help someone else. To be a living sacrifice means we give up our own will and way—things that are important to most people—to do things God's way while we live on this earth.

[And, friend, being a living sacrifice is going to be one of the hardest things you'll ever do.]

SKG
Puzzle Craze

Unscramble these words.

ILVGIN   ACSFCIERI

_____

_____

We must become living sacrifices. This is hard because we have two choices. We can let our bodies' desires direct our lives, or we can let God's Spirit direct our lives. (Remember that battle between our flesh and our spirit that we learned about earlier?) Campus Crusade for Christ has developed these drawings to help us understand the concept of a living sacrifice.[3] Under the diagram labeled number 1, write "Unbeliever." Under the diagram labeled number 2, write "Unsacrificial Christian." Under the diagram labeled number 3, write "Living Sacrifice."

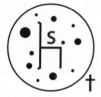 

1._____ **2.** _____ **3.** _____

Which circle is most orderly? _____

Which two are most out of order? _____ and _____

What do you think the "S" might stand for in these two? _____
(*Hint: It's the root of the word "selfish."*)

The circle represents a person's life. Anything inside the circle is a part of their life. In the first circle, is Jesus in the person's life at all?_____

The chair, or throne, represents the seat of power and authority in a person's life. Who is on that seat in the second circle? _____

In the second circle, Jesus is in the person's life. Why isn't there more order? _____

_____

When you are on the throne of your life (when you think you are "the boss"), your life is not in order, and you can't live like God's kid. Having self on the throne is called "living according to the flesh." But when Jesus is on that throne, you can truly honor God with your body. That is called "living according to the Spirit," or being a "living sacrifice," because everything you do is for Christ.

This is probably a good time for us to tell you that Jesus loves you no matter what your circle looks like. He doesn't love people only if they have done a lot for him. He loves all people—from inside the womb until they die—no matter what. But we will find more peace and joy in our lives by being living sacrifices.

Look Inside Yourself

Let's take just one part of our body to learn what it means to be a living sacrifice. We've selected our mouths because they seem to get us into a lot of trouble when we are in charge of them. There are a bunch of proverbs that say a foolish person uses her mouth way too much. Has it ever occurred to you that *not* saying something could be a way to exercise self-control, a way to be a living sacrifice, and a way to glorify God?

THINK ABOUT IT

In what way do each of these things bring honor to God?

1. keeping a secret _____

2. not repeating gossip _____

3. counting to ten when angry _____

4. asking someone about their day instead of talking about yours

_____

The ways we can honor God with our speech (or our silence) are nearly endless! When we are children, the Bible says in 1 Corinthians 13:11, we speak, act, and reason like children. Little children have to learn how to control their speech because they tend to be a bit loud, they repeat things they have been told not to, and they don't worry too much about unkindness. They will say the most inappropriate things at the most inappropriate times!

The other day my (Suzy's) two-year-old grandson had to be taken out of church because he had just learned that church is God's house...and he would not stop shouting during worship, "This is God's house! This is God's house!" He spoke truth, but not at the right time—and definitely not at the right volume level! You would not do that because you have learned to control your mouth in situations like that. But are you ever guilty of lacking self-control and sacrifice when it comes to your tongue? We are. Confess this right now by writing a list of things you need to work on. (You might use the list above to get ideas.)

1. _____

2. _____

3. _____

4. _____

5. _____

Keep a close watch on your mouth for the next couple of days. Are you unkind with your words? Are you loud? Do you say more than you need to? Practice being a living sacrifice with just this one part of your body.

Reach Up to Talk to GoD

Dear Jesus,

I'm ready to talk about the throne of my life. Am I the boss, or are you? Right now, I think I'm living as if the boss is _____ **(insert a name—yours, Jesus', or maybe even someone else's!).** I know that unless you are on that throne, things are just going to be a mess! Here are some things I've really let you be the boss of: _____

_____. But here are some ways I'm listening to myself instead of listening to you:

_____

_____. This world says that I should follow my heart, that I should do what's good for me, that I have to take care of myself and love myself, or I can never love anyone else. But you say I always have to put you and others ahead of me. I want to do that. I honor you with my body when I do that. I want my hands to _____. I want my mouth to _____. I want my feet to _____. And most of all, I want my knees to bow down before you, the one who sits on the throne forever and ever!

Answers to Puzzle Crazes

Answer to puzzle on page 15:

```
H
O        D
U        W
S        E
T E M P L E
         L
         I
         N
         G
```

Answer to puzzle on page 26:

Mary was a virgin and not married yet to **Joseph**. God used **Mary** to create Jesus' body, but he did not use Joseph; Mary became **pregnant** by a miracle of God's **Holy** Spirit. Jesus was born in **Bethlehem**, which was not his parents' hometown. Because there was no **room** for the family anywhere in town, **Jesus** was born and laid in a **manger**. **Angels** informed the **shepherds** of the birth by saying, **"Glory** to God in the highest." The shepherds were fast learners because pretty soon they were **glorifying** God.

Answer to puzzle on page 67:

Gray hair is a crown of glory; it is gained in a righteous life.

Answer to puzzle on page 69:

	Legalism	A Fair Judgment	God's Real Rules
JEN	☹		
SARAH		☺	
ALISON			☺

Answer to puzzle on page 82:

```
                              C
                              A
                              R
                              R
      T     R     B           O
      O     I     L     P     T
   W  A  T  E  R  M  E  L  O  N  S
      T     C     B     A
      T           E     T
      O           R     O
   P  E  A  S     R     E
      S           Y     S
```

Answer to puzzle on page 42:

```
E G D C W G B E V K N B S N D
D X E M Y Y L X R F W K B A B
Y K M M S A E Z T P T U P K Q
L A R J M E R H C S C B V O S
Y B O E Y R B Z I H C M D G N
R J F E Y A X L X D P B U H D
D B S J N E P X L Z Q S N Q M
D T N T V I J O Z E E S X P U
S V A O Y H M F H J J D D I D
A C R S D U P A X F Z C I A H
F E T H K L C B G Y M M K I U
F O V O K T D J G E A T X W H
E C H A D C R N U L L K D Z I
T L Y U K L L X M L E F T N N
J K P M B P N V N Z G X G L I
```

Answer to puzzle on page 106:

```
V Q C U I G N C D E V O C B P
G B O D Y S P R A Y H A L T R
L O D I M F T Z P E S T U K Z
Z D R S Q A R R G B Z O U B G
W M R B M M Z U N H Z R X W E
Y N A P R D N L I X K Z D T P
E L O X E Q J D T E L H A Q G
A N L M I R V H A T U L N L B
S W S I X P T Y E F O E T P Q
G T Z N G A A R H C V F B H C
P S E I E H G D O C H Q K F E
N I Y P W U H H S W B U D Y C
D W X A C V C E B L P S E D M
E S F D Q W F E M M D B W F S
Q V U S B O G E X E E I A K W
```

NOTES

4: Your Hair, a Crown

1. Photo of Carolina Turbyfill is by Meghan Taylor Photography.

2. We've wanted to write about legalism as it refers to beauty, modesty, and fashion for a long time. We've chosen this book because it seems like talking about the body mandates we address legalistic standards concerning it. We've chosen this chapter because few people are likely to disagree with what we have to say about God's guidelines for hair.

8: Your Body, a Sacrifice

3. Bill Bright, *Have You Made the Wonderful Discovery of the Spirit-Filled Life?* (Peachtree City, GA: Campus Crusade for Christ, 1966). Used by permission.